Scraps & Stash Quilting™

Editor **Carolyn S. Vagts**
Creative Director **Brad Snow**
Publishing Services Director **Brenda Gallmeyer**

Managing Editor **Barb Sprunger**
Graphic Designer **Nick Pierce**
Copy Supervisor **Corene Painter**
Senior Copy Editor **Emily Carter**
Technical Editors **Angie Buckles, Sandra L. Hatch**
Technical Artist **Debera Kuntz**

Production Artist Supervisor **Erin Brandt**
Production Artists **Nicole Gage, Debera Kuntz**
Production Assistants **Marj Morgan,**
                Judy Neuenschwander

Photography Supervisor **Tammy Christian**
Photography **Matthew Owen**
Photography Assistants **Tammy Liechty,**
                Tammy Steiner

Scraps & Stash Quilting is published by Annie's, 306 East Parr Road, Berne, IN 46711. Printed in USA. Copyright © 2013 Annie's. All rights reserved. This publication may not be reproduced in part or in whole without written permission from the publisher.

RETAIL STORES: If you would like to carry this pattern book or any other Annie's publications, visit AnniesWSL.com

Every effort has been made to ensure that the instructions in this publication are complete and accurate. We cannot, however, take responsibility for human error, typographical mistakes or variations in individual work. Please visit AnniesCustomerCare.com to check for pattern updates.

Library of Congress Control Number: 2012954172
ISBN: 978-1-59635-800-3
Printed in the USA

1 2 3 4 5 6 7 8 9 10

Welcome

Scraps and stash, for a quilter, are inevitable. If you quilt, you have scraps. Another side effect of quilting is collecting a stash. Quilters are drawn to beautiful fabrics like moths to light bulbs. A great thing about scraps and stash is that you probably selected them originally, so you should love them.

If you think of scrap projects as a collection of all the fabrics you truly love, it takes on new meaning. Imagine all your favorite fabrics in one quilt. It has got to be great.

This book contains more than 38 quilting ideas you can make with scraps and stash. There's everything from small projects, like pincushions and backpacks, to queen-size bed quilts. There's something for everyone in all sizes and all skill levels. *Scraps & Stash Quilting* is a must for every quilter. It will become the classic go-to book when you need a gift or inspiration. Explore your options with these timeless designs. Your fabrics will make them exactly what you're looking for.

Our hope is that you find many fun scrappy projects in this book that will inspire you to dive into your scraps and stash and turn them into meaningful and useful quilts and gifts. Put your fabric resources to work.

Carolyn S. Vagts

Contents

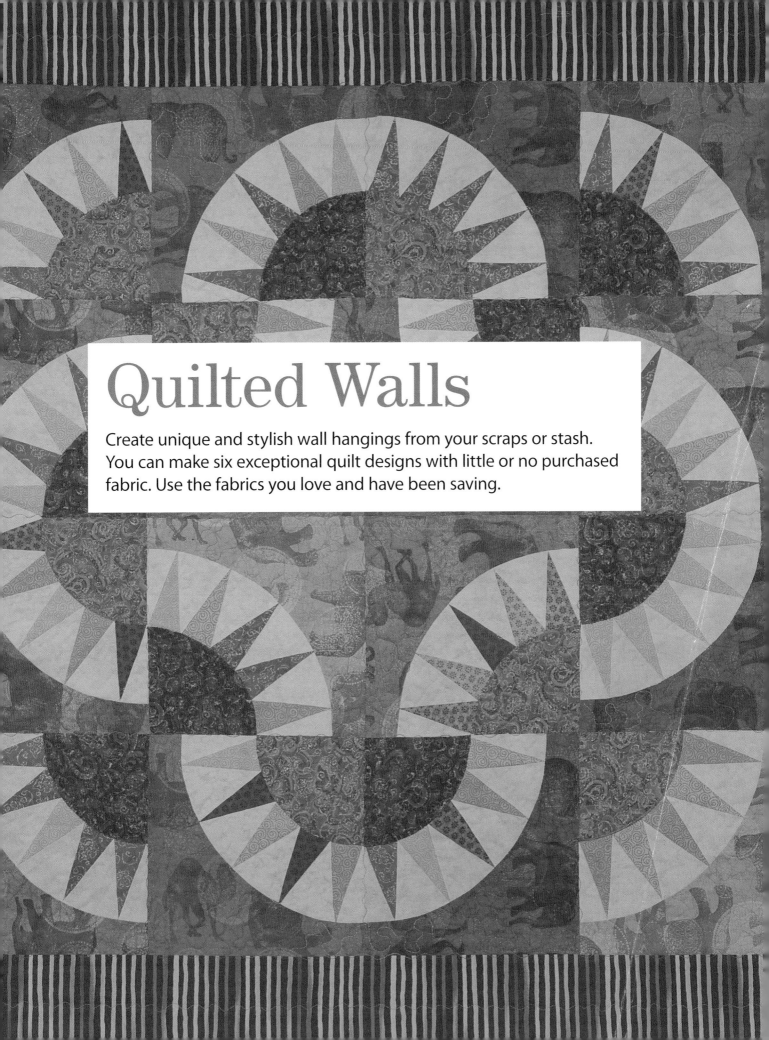

Quilted Walls

Create unique and stylish wall hangings from your scraps or stash. You can make six exceptional quilt designs with little or no purchased fabric. Use the fabrics you love and have been saving.

Burst of Color

Bright-colored scraps combine with a colorful stripe in this stunning wall quilt.

DESIGN BY DEBBY KRATOVIL

PROJECT SPECIFICATIONS

Skill Level: Intermediate
Quilt Size: 37" x 37"
Block Size: 7" x 7"
Number of Blocks: 16

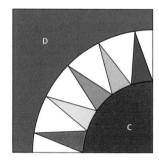

Burst of Color
7" x 7" Block
Make 16

MATERIALS

Assorted bright-colored scraps
¼ yard each red and blue/purple prints
⅓ yard each red, purple, blue and green tonals and
    gold/orange print
⅜ yard green tonal
⅔ yard black/bright-colored stripe
¾ yard cream tonal
Backing 43" x 43"
Batting 43" x 43"
Thread
Paper piecing material
Basic sewing tools and supplies

Cutting

1. Cut 80 (1¾" x 3½") B rectangles from the assorted bright-colored scraps.

2. Prepare templates for C; cut as directed on patterns from red and blue/purple prints.

3. Prepare templates for D; cut as directed on patterns from red, purple, blue and green tonals and gold/orange print.

4. Cut four 2¼" by fabric width green tonal strips for binding.

5. Cut four 5" x 40" black/bright-colored stripe E strips.

6. Cut six 3½" by fabric width cream tonal strips; subcut 96 (2½" x 3½") A rectangles.

Completing the Blocks

1. Prepare 16 copies of the curved paper-piecing pattern.

2. Place an A right side up on the unmarked side of the paper, covering section 1 and extending at least ¼" into all surrounding areas. Place a B piece right sides together with A on the 1-2 seam side as shown in Figure 1; turn paper over and stitch on the marked 1-2 line.

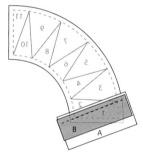

Figure 1

3. Trim excess seam allowance to extend ¼" beyond the 2-3 line; press B to the right side as shown in Figure 2.

Figure 2

4. Continue adding A and B pieces in numerical order in this manner until entire paper foundation is covered.

5. Trim finished unit along outside-edge line to complete an A-B unit; repeat to complete 16 A-B units.

6. Mark the center on the wrong side of each C and D piece as marked on templates.

7. To complete one Burst of Color block, sew C to the A-B unit, matching centers and clipping into curves as necessary to fit as shown in Figure 3; press seams toward the A-B unit.

Figure 3

8. Repeat step 7, sewing the A-B-C unit to D to complete one block; press seam toward D. Remove paper foundation.

9. Repeat steps 7 and 8 to complete 16 Burst of Color blocks referring to the Placement Diagram for color placement of C and D pieces in blocks.

Completing the Quilt

1. Arrange and join four Burst of Color blocks to make an X row referring to Figure 4 and the Placement Diagram; press seams in one direction. Repeat to make two X rows referring to the Placement Diagram for positioning of colors.

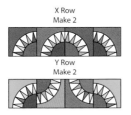

X Row
Make 2

Y Row
Make 2

Figure 4

2. Repeat step 1 with four Burst of Color blocks to make two Y rows, again referring to Figure 4 and the Placement Diagram; press seams in one direction.

3. Referring to the Placement Diagram for positioning of rows, arrange and join the X and Y rows to complete the pieced center.

4. Fold each E strip and crease to mark the centers.

5. Pin and stitch E strips to each side of the pieced center, matching centers and stopping stitching ¼" from each end of the pieced center.

6. Fold strips at each corner at a 45-degree angle, matching stripes as shown in Figure 5; press to mark seam line and pin to hold. Stitch corner seams on creased lines, again referring to Figure 5 to make a mitered corner; trim seam to ¼" and press mitered seams open and border seams toward E to complete the pieced top.

Figure 5

7. Layer, quilt and bind referring to Finishing Your Quilt on page 160. ■

Burst of Color
Placement Diagram 37" x 37"

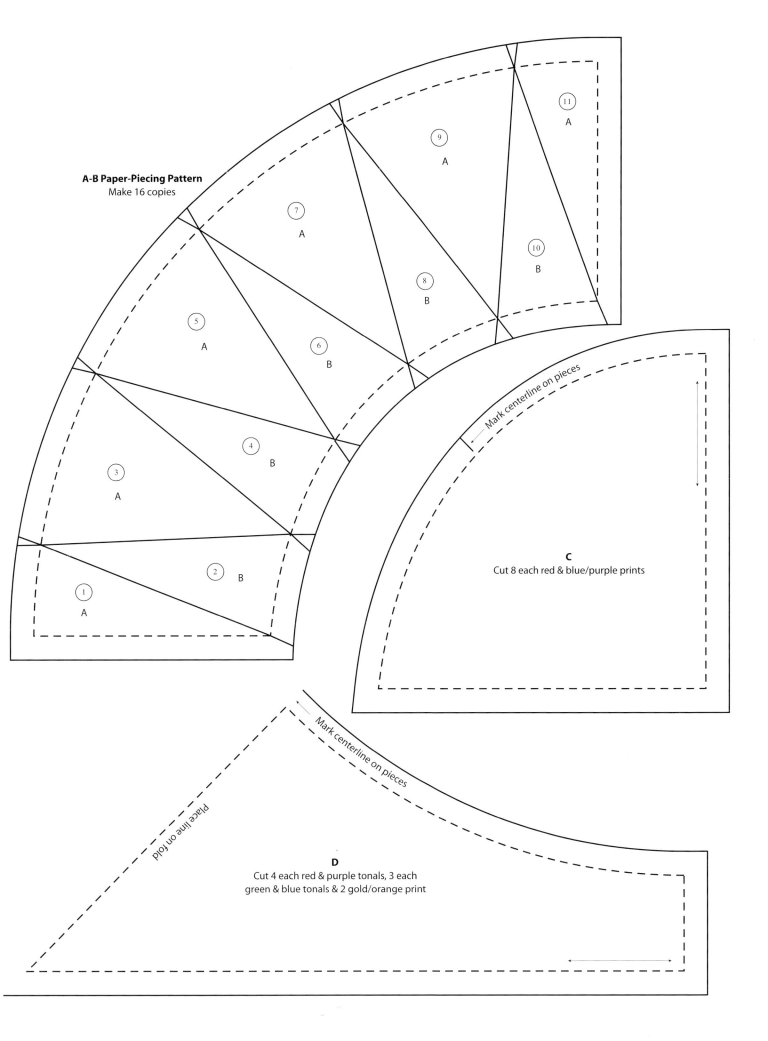

A-B Paper-Piecing Pattern
Make 16 copies

⑦ A

⑤ A

⑨ A

⑪ A

⑩ B

⑧ B

⑥ B

③ A

④ B

② B

① A

Mark centerline on pieces

C
Cut 8 each red & blue/purple prints

Mark centerline on pieces

Place line on fold

D
Cut 4 each red & purple tonals, 3 each
green & blue tonals & 2 gold/orange print

Gettysburg Revisited

A perfect tribute to a time gone by. Update with your stash to match your decor or leave it just as it is. This is a great HST (half-square triangle) project.

DESIGN BY CONNIE KAUFFMAN

PROJECT SPECIFICATIONS

Skill Level: Beginner
Quilt Size: 39½" x 39½"
Block Size: 6" x 6"
Number of Blocks: 9

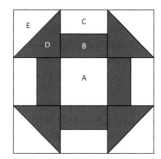

Hole in the Barn Door
6" x 6" Block
Make 9

MATERIALS

⅜ yard each tan, black and blue leaf prints
⅜ yard each 9 red, blue and brown prints
½ yard gold print
¾ yard cream print
Backing 48" x 48"
Batting 48" x 48"
Thread
Triangle paper (optional)
Basic sewing tools and supplies

PROJECT NOTES

Using a product such as Triangle Papers by Quiltime to make the half-square triangle units means you can use 2½"-wide strips to create the units.

Cutting

1. Cut four 2¼" by fabric width tan strips; subcut two each 2¼" x 27½" K and 2¼" x 31" L strips.

2. Cut eight 1¼" by fabric width black strips; subcut two each 1¼" x 26" I, 1¼" x 27½" J, 1¼" x 31" M and 1¼" x 32½" N strips.

3. Cut four 2¼" by fabric width blue leaf print strips; subcut two each 2¼" x 36½" P and 2¼" x 40" Q strips.

4. From each of nine red, blue and brown prints, cut four 1½" x 2½" B rectangles and six 2⅞" D squares.

5. From each of four red, blue and brown prints, cut one 6½" F square.

6. From one of the red, blue or brown prints, cut four 2½" O squares.

7. Prepare templates for G and H pieces using patterns given; cut as directed on each piece from the remainder of the red, blue and brown prints.

8. Cut five 2¼" by fabric width gold print strips for binding.

9. Cut two 2½" by fabric width cream print strips; subcut nine 2½" A squares and 36 (1½" x 2½") C rectangles.

10. Cut four 2⅞" by fabric width cream print strips; subcut 50 (2⅞") E squares.

Completing the Blocks

1. Draw a diagonal line from corner to corner on the wrong side of each E square.

2. Place an E square right sides together with a D square and stitch ¼" on each side of the marked line as shown in Figure 1.

Figure 1

3. Cut the stitched unit apart on the marked line to make two triangle units as shown in Figure 2; press seams toward D to complete two D-E half-square triangle units.

Figure 2

4. Repeat steps 2 and 3 to complete a total of 100 D-E units. ***Note:*** *You will have four extra D squares; set these aside for another project.*

5. To complete one Hole in the Barn Door block, select four matching B rectangles, four matching D-E units, four C rectangles and one A square.

6. Sew B and then C to opposite sides of A to make the center row as shown in Figure 3; press seams toward B.

Figure 3

7. Sew B to C to make a B-C unit; repeat to make a second B-C unit.

8. Sew a D-E unit to opposite ends of a B-C unit to make the top row as shown in Figure 4; press seams toward the B-C unit. Repeat to make the bottom row.

Figure 4

9. Sew a top and bottom row to opposite sides of the center row to complete one Hole in the Barn Door block as shown in Figure 5; press seams toward the center row.

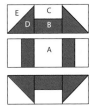

Figure 5

10. Repeat steps 5–9 to complete a total of nine Hole in the Barn Door blocks.

Completing the Quilt

1. Arrange and join the blocks with the F squares and G and H triangles in diagonal rows and corner units referring to Figure 6; press seams away from the blocks.

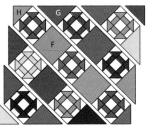

Figure 6

2. Join the rows and corner units as arranged to complete the pieced center; press seams in one direction.

3. Sew I strips to the top and bottom and J strips to opposite sides of the pieced center; press seams toward I and J strips.

4. Repeat step 3 with K and L strips; press seams toward K and L.

5. Repeat step 3 with M and N strips; press seams toward M and N.

6. Select eight different D-E units and join to make a D-E strip as shown in Figure 7; press seams in one direction. Repeat to make a total of four D-E strips and four reversed D-E strips, again referring to Figure 7.

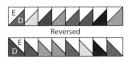

Figure 7

7. Join one each D-E and reversed D-E strips to make a side strip as shown in Figure 8; press seam to one side. Repeat to make a total of four side strips.

Figure 8

8. Sew a side strip to opposite sides of the pieced center; press seams toward N strips.

9. Sew an O square to each end of each remaining side strip and sew to the top and bottom of the pieced center; press seams toward O and then toward M strips.

10. Sew P strips to the top and bottom and Q strips to opposite sides of the pieced center; press seams toward P and Q strips to complete the pieced top.

11. Layer, quilt and bind referring to Finishing Your Quilt on page 160. ■

Gettysburg Revisited
Placement Diagram 39½" x 39½"

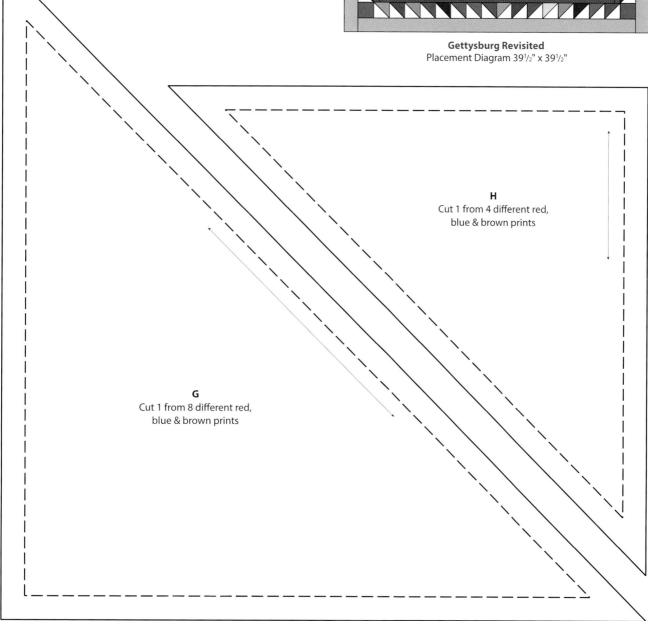

H
Cut 1 from 4 different red,
blue & brown prints

G
Cut 1 from 8 different red,
blue & brown prints

Rules of Chaos

The Rules of Chaos quilts are influenced by the vibrant colors and simple, stark geometry of traditional and antique Amish quilts.

DESIGNS BY CYNTHIA MYERBERG

PROJECT NOTES

Traditional quiltmaking requires strict adherence to measurements, methods of construction and use of templates. I choose to bend the rules. Free-form cutting and an improvisational approach to design give the resulting quilts a more fluid, organic look than their predecessors. Geometric forms are mixed, skewed and stretched. I hand-dyed all of the 100 percent cotton fabrics that make up the quilts. I strive for uneven hues that simulate the patina of the antique quilts by folding and crumpling the fabric in the dye bath, often achieving a suede-like surface. Contemporary quiltmaking tools and ideas bring these quilts into the 21st century. Assembly and quilting are done by machine.

For freehand-cutting Rules of Chaos quilts, the shapes and strips are cut slightly larger than for a conventional quilt because you need to overlap each piece and cut it to fit.

RULES OF CHAOS #8

PROJECT SPECIFICATIONS

Skill Level: Intermediate
Quilt Size: Approximately 21" x 56"
Block Size: Approximately 7" x 7"
Number of Blocks: 24

Rules of Chaos #8
Approximately 7" x 7" Block

MATERIALS

Scraps of a variety of hand-dyed fabrics in light and dark values
1¼ yards black solid
Backing 27" x 62"
Batting 27" x 62"
Thread
Basic sewing tools and supplies

Piecing Free-Form Blocks

1. Use a rotary cutter to freehand-cut a rectangle approximately 4½" x 3" for A. Do not try to make it a perfect rectangle, but give it a slightly lopsided shape as shown in Figure 1. **Note:** *If your rectangle is considerably smaller than the recommended size, make the surrounding strips wider to make up the difference. A variety in the size of the rectangles and strips gives this quilt a more contemporary look.*

Figure 1

2. Freehand-cut a contrasting fabric in strips approximately 1¾"–2¼" wide for B and C. Label the narrower strips B and the wider strips C.

3. Lay the long edge of A next to a B strip and cut B at least ½" longer than A. Overlap the edges of A and B slightly as shown in Figure 2.

Figure 2

4. Using the edge of A as a guide, cut the strip along the edge of A following the shape suggested by A as shown in Figure 3. ***Note:*** *Do not square off these strips, but rather, follow the shape of the block.* Sew B to A; press seam to one side. Trim B ends even with A.

Figure 3

5. Lay the top edge of the A-B unit next to a C strip. Slightly overlap the edges. Using the edge of the A-B unit as a guide, cut the C strip along the edge of A-B as shown in Figure 4. Trim off ends to follow the shape of the block and sew C to the A-B unit; press seams to one side.

Figure 4

6. Continue to build the block in this manner until you have surrounded the center A with the contrasting fabric, using wider C strips for the top and bottom of the rectangle and narrower B strips for the sides as shown in Figure 5.

Figure 5

7. Freehand-cut black solid strips approximately 2¼" wide. Cut two strips at least ½" longer than the sides of the pieced unit. Lay the long edge of the pieced unit next to a black strip, slightly overlapping the strip. Using the edge of the rectangle as a guide, cut the strip along the edge of the rectangle. Sew on the black strip.

8. Repeat this process on the other side of the pieced unit as shown in Figure 6; press seam to one side. Trim off ends to follow the shape of the block.

Figure 6

9. Measure the block; it should be a rectangular shape. Don't worry about the exact size and don't trim anything until you are ready to assemble the quilt.

10. Repeat the process to make 24 blocks that are close to the same size.

Completing the Top

1. Arrange the pieced blocks on a design wall until the color placement is pleasing.

2. Lay out the first row of three blocks on your cutting surface referring to Figure 7, lining up according to size. ***Note:*** *If all three blocks are approximately the same size, you have been lucky.* Overlap one block over the black strip of the second block and cut using the top block as a guide.

Figure 7

3. Sew the two blocks together; press seams in one direction. ***Note:*** *If one block is longer/shorter than the other, leave it for now. Don't trim off excess until you are ready to join the rows.*

4. Place row 2 on the cutting surface; line up blocks as shown in Figure 8. Overlap, cut, sew and press as in steps 2 and 3. Repeat for all rows.

Figure 8

5. Lay rows 1 and 2 on the cutting surface. Line up the rows, centering the center blocks. ***Note:*** *Don't worry if seams don't meet.* Freehand-trim the bottom edge of the top row as shown in Figure 9, remembering that these should not be too straight, but slightly curved. Sew row 1 to row 2; press seam to one side.

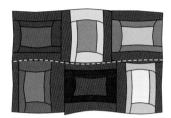

Figure 9

6. Continue sewing one row to the next in the same manner until the top is complete; press seams in one direction.

7. When the top is complete, freehand-trim around the entire piece, trimming all uneven edges.

Finishing the Quilt

1. Layer and quilt referring to Finishing Your Quilt on page 160.

2. When quilting is complete, trim batting and backing edges even with the quilted top.

3. Prepare 4¾ yards black solid bias binding and bind edges of quilt to finish. ***Note:*** *The binding should be made of bias strips because the edges of the quilt are not perfectly straight and require some curved stitching.*

RULES OF CHAOS #9

PROJECT NOTE

This quilt is made using the same methods as Rules of Chaos #8 except that the blocks are almost square before they are cut in half and rearranged to create a whole new look.

PROJECT SPECIFICATIONS

Skill Level: Intermediate
Quilt Size: 28" x 44"
Block Size: Approximately 8" x 8"
Number of Blocks: 15

Rules of Chaos #9
Approximately 8" x 8" Block

MATERIALS

Scraps of a variety of hand-dyed fabrics in light and
   dark values
1¼ yards black solid
Backing 34" x 50"
Batting 34" x 50"
Neutral color all-purpose thread
Quilting thread
Basic sewing tools and supplies

Making Blocks

1. Freehand-cut strips of light and dark fabrics and black solid 1½", 1¾", 2", 2¼" and 2½" wide.

2. Freehand-cut squares that are approximately 2½", 3½" and 4" square. ***Note:*** *Use a variety of sizes of squares and strips to create visual interest.*

3. Begin with any square and a different-color strip; sew the strip to the square referring to Piecing Free-Form Blocks for Rules of Chaos #8. Continue to add strips around the square referring to Figure 10 for order of piecing. ***Note:*** *For consistent-size blocks, use the following formula: 4" square with 1½" and 2¼" strips; 3½" square with 1¾" and 2¼" strips; 2½" square with 2" and 2½" strips.*

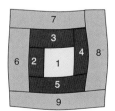

Figure 10

4. Measure the finished block and trim to 9" x 9". Repeat to make 15 blocks.

Completing the Top

1. Freehand-cut each block in half as shown in Figure 11.

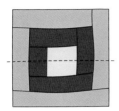

Figure 11

2. Pair the cut half-blocks and arrange in five rows of three pairs each referring to Figure 12 for one row. Move block halves around until you are satisfied with the arrangement.

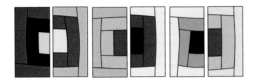

Figure 12

3. Join half-blocks to make squares as shown in Figure 13; trim blocks to 8½" x 8½" to make square again after stitching, keeping center seam centered.

Figure 13

4. Lay the blocks out in rows again and join to make a row; repeat for five rows. Press seams in adjacent rows in opposite directions. Join the rows to complete the pieced center; press seams in one direction.

5. Cut two 2½" x 40½" A strips and two 2½" x 28½" B strips black solid. Sew A to opposite long sides and B to the top and bottom of the pieced center; press seams toward strips.

Finishing the Quilt

1. Finish referring to Finishing the Quilt instructions for Rules of Chaos #8 except make 4½ yards black bias binding. ■

Rules of Chaos #9
Placement Diagram
28" x 44"

Concrete Jungle

Add some interest to any wall with this engaging quilt.

DESIGN BY GINA GEMPESAW

PROJECT SPECIFICATIONS

Skill Level: Confident Beginner
Wall Hanging Size: 32" x 20¼"

MATERIALS

26 assorted precut 5" squares
⅓ yard coordinating dark tonal
⅓ yard gray tonal
⅝ yard cream tonal
Backing 40" x 28"
Batting 40" x 28"
Neutral-color all-purpose thread
Quilting thread
Basic sewing tools and supplies

Cutting

1. Trim each of nine 5" precut squares to 2⅞" square; cut each one in half on one diagonal to make 18 C triangles. Set aside one triangle of each fabric for another project.

2. Trim each of two 5" precut squares to 3¼" square; cut each one on both diagonals to make a total of eight E triangles. Set aside three triangles of each fabric for another project.

3. Cut each of the remaining 5" precut squares into four 2½" A squares to total 60 A squares. Set aside three squares for another project. *Note: For more variety, use additional precut squares to make more A squares; choose 57 squares for wall hanging and save extra squares for other projects.*

4. Cut two 2½" by fabric width strips gray tonal; subcut strips into 68 (¾" x 2½") B pieces.

5. Cut two 1" by fabric width strips gray tonal; subcut each strip into two 1" x 20¾" G strips to total four G strips.

6. Cut one 3¼" by fabric width strip cream tonal; subcut strip into one 3¼" square. Cut the square on both diagonals to make four F triangles; set aside two triangles.

7. Trim the remainder of the cream tonal 3¼" strip to 2⅞" and cut six 2⅞" squares; subcut each square in half on one diagonal to make a total of 12 D triangles. Set aside one triangle.

8. Cut four 1½" by fabric width strips cream tonal; cut each strip into two 1½" x 20¾" H strips to total eight H strips.

9. Cut two 2½" by fabric width strips cream tonal. From each strip, subcut one each of the following sizes: 2½" x 7¼" J, 2½" x 2¾" K, 2½" x 9½" L and 2½" x 5" M. Cut the remainder of strips into one each of the following sizes: 2½" x 14" N and 2½" x 11¾" O.

10. Cut three 2¼" by fabric width strips coordinating dark tonal for binding.

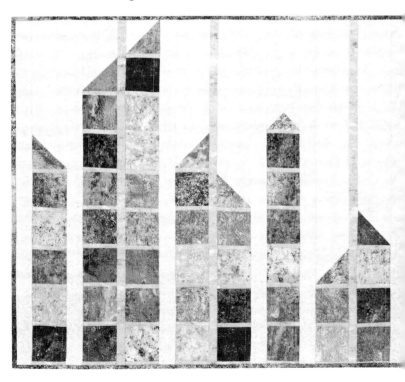

Completing the Quilt

1. Select one each C and D triangle; join along the diagonal to make a C-D unit as shown in Figure 1; press seam toward C. Repeat to make a total of nine C-D units.

Make 9

Figure 1

Make 2

Figure 2

2. Select one each E and F triangle; join along one short edge of F to make one E-F unit as shown in Figure 2; press seam toward E. Repeat to make a total of two E-F units.

3. Sew a D triangle to an E-F unit as shown in Figure 3 to make one D-E-F unit. Repeat to make a second D-E-F unit.

Make 2

Figure 3

Make 57

Figure 4

4. Sew a B strip to one side of an A square to make one A-B unit as shown in Figure 4; press seam toward B. Repeat to make a total of 57 A-B units.

5. Arrange and join five A-B units, one B piece and one C-D unit with J to make row 1 as shown in Figure 5; press seams in one direction.

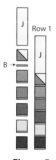

Figure 5

6. Repeat step 5 with the remaining pieced units and B pieces, adding J, K, L, M, N or O strips to the ends of the joined units to complete the remaining rows as shown in Figure 6; press seams in one direction in each row.

7. Join rows 2 and 3 with a G strip as shown in Figure 7; press seams toward G. Repeat with rows 4 and 5, rows 7 and 8, and rows 9 and 10, again referring to Figure 6. Press seams toward G strips.

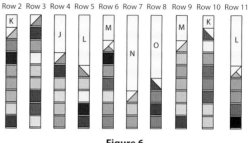

Figure 6

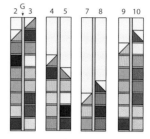

Figure 7

8. Arrange and join the rows with the H strips referring to Figure 8 to complete the pieced top; press seams toward H strips.

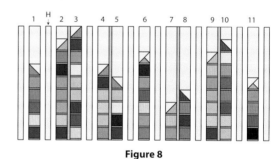

Figure 8

9. Layer, quilt and bind referring to Finishing Your Quilt on page 160. ■

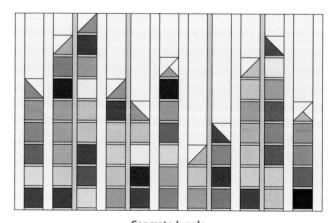

Concrete Jungle
Placement Diagram 32" x 20¼"

African Sunset

The animals gather around to enjoy this fabric rendition of an African sunset.

DESIGN BY LUCY A. FAZELY & MICHAEL L. BURNS

PROJECT SPECIFICATIONS

Skill Level: Confident Beginner
Quilt Size: 30" x 30"

MATERIALS

9" square blue batik
10" square each of 5 different green batiks
¾ yard sunset batik
1¼ yards black batik
Backing 36" x 36"
Batting 36" x 36"
Black all-purpose thread
Variegated green machine-quilting thread
Clear nylon monofilament
2 yards 12"-wide fusible web
2 yards 20"-wide fabric stabilizer
Basting spray
Basic sewing tools and supplies

Cutting

1. Cut four 3½" by fabric width black batik strips; subcut two each 3½" x 24½" A strips and 3½" x 30½" B strips.

2. Cut four 2¼" by fabric width strips black batik for binding.

3. Prepare templates for appliqué shapes using patterns given; trace shapes on the paper side of the fusible web referring to patterns for number to cut and leaving at least ½" between shapes. ***Note:*** *Patterns have been given in reverse for fusible appliqué.*

4. Cut around shapes, leaving a margin around each one; fuse to the wrong sides of fabrics as directed on patterns for color. Cut out shapes on traced lines; remove paper backing.

5. Cut a 24½" square sunset batik for background.

Completing the Quilt

1. Fold and crease background square vertically, horizontally and diagonally to mark the center as shown in Figure 1.

Figure 1

2. Center the Earth circle on the background using crease lines as guides; fuse center only in place, leaving edges free to tuck animal feet under. Place the Africa and Madagascar shapes on the Earth; pin in place.

3. Center the antelopes on the horizontal and vertical lines with about ¼" of their feet tucked under the Earth. Center the giraffes on the diagonal lines, tucking feet under as for antelopes. Fuse all pieces in place.

4. Cut fabric stabilizer pieces to fit behind the entire fused background; pin in place.

5. Using clear nylon monofilament in the top of the machine and matching all-purpose thread in the bobbin, machine-appliqué around all edges of the fused shapes using a narrow satin stitch. ***Note:*** *All appliqué stitching on the sample was done with a 1.5 stitch width and a .6 stitch length.*

6. Sew A strips to opposite sides and B strips to the top and bottom of the pieced center; press seams toward strips.

7. Arrange the leaves on opposite corners referring to the Placement Diagram for positioning suggestions. When satisfied with arrangement, fuse shapes in place.

8. Load green variegated thread in the top of the machine and black all-purpose thread in the bobbin and machine-stitch a narrow zigzag line for all stems and around all leaf shapes. ***Note:*** *All stem stitching done with 1.5 stitch width and .4 stitch length. Remove fabric stabilizer.*

9. Layer, quilt and bind referring to Finishing Your Quilt on page 160, using basting spray to hold layers together, and machine-quilting and craft thread for quilting. ◼

African Sunset
Placement Diagram
30" x 30"

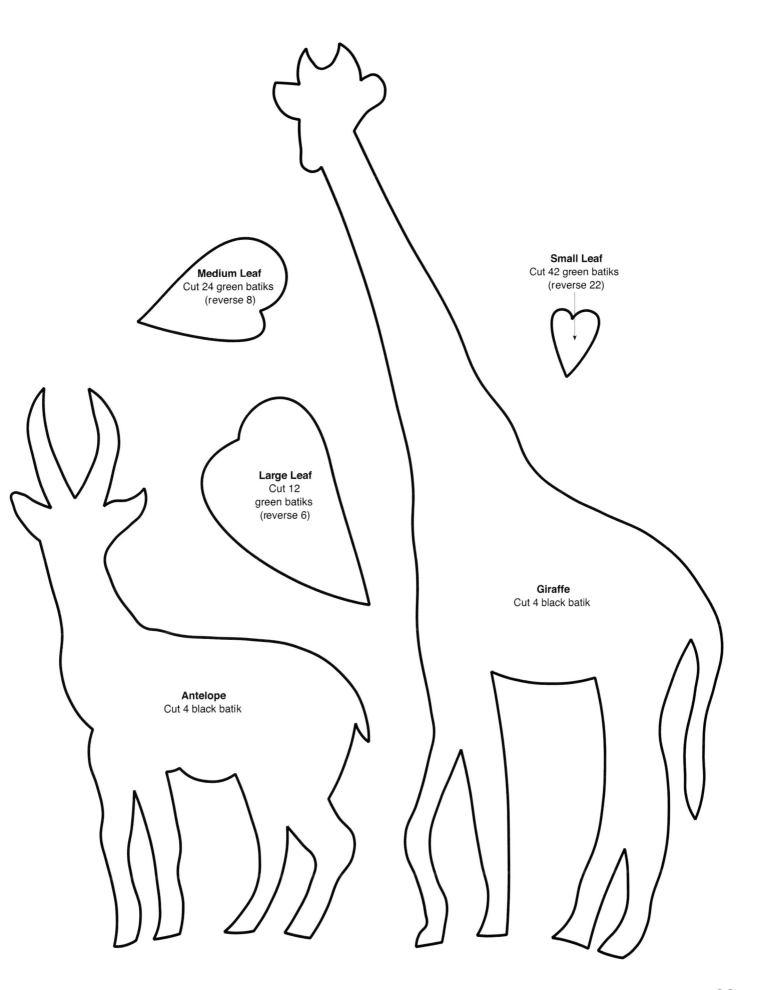

Medium Leaf
Cut 24 green batiks
(reverse 8)

Small Leaf
Cut 42 green batiks
(reverse 22)

Large Leaf
Cut 12
green batiks
(reverse 6)

Giraffe
Cut 4 black batik

Antelope
Cut 4 black batik

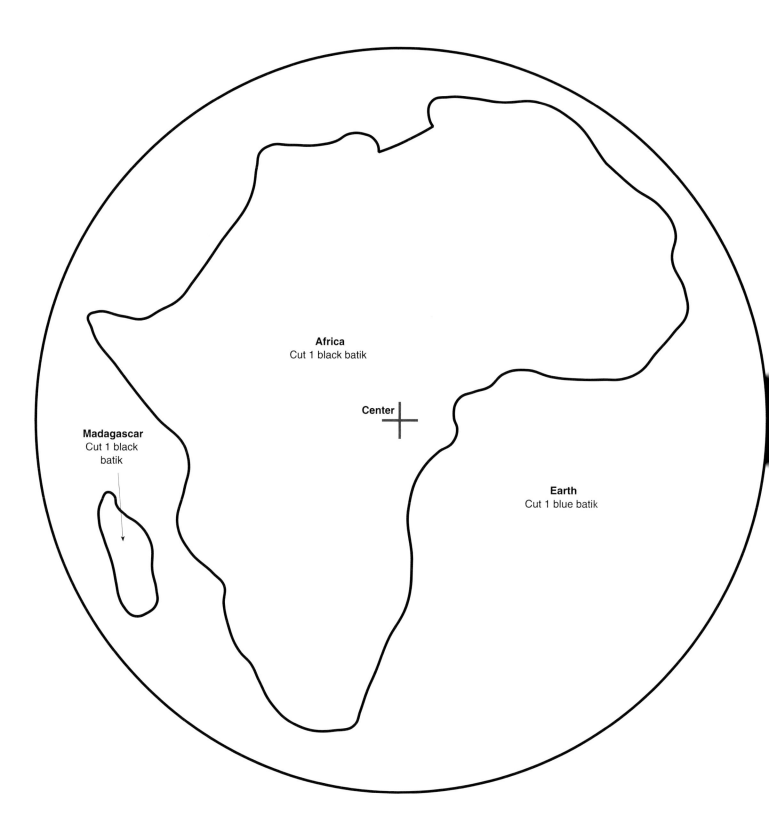

Africa
Cut 1 black batik

Center

Madagascar
Cut 1 black
batik

Earth
Cut 1 blue batik

The Romance of Camelot

Dress up this quick-to-stitch wall quilt with beaded trim.

DESIGN BY CHERYL ADAM

PROJECT SPECIFICATIONS

Skill Level: Intermediate
Quilt Size: 42" x 64"
Unit Size: 6" x 3"
Number of Units: 105

MATERIALS

51 print 3½" x 6½" A rectangles
54 solid 3½" x 6½" C rectangles
108 print 3½" D squares
102 solid 3½" B squares
1 yard purple solid
Backing 44" x 66"
Batting 44" x 66"
Thread
1½ yards beaded trim
Basic sewing tools and supplies

Cutting

1. Cut five 3½" by fabric width purple solid strips. Subcut six 3½" x 6½" E rectangles and five 3½" F squares from two of the strips.

2. Join remaining three purple solid strips on short ends to make one long strip. Subcut strip into one 3½" x 48½" H strip and one 3½" x 63½" G strip.

3. Cut one 1½" x 42½" I strip purple solid.

Piecing Flying Geese Units

1. Mark a line from corner to corner on the wrong side of all B and D squares.

2. Referring to Figure 1, place a B square on each end of A; stitch on the marked lines. Trim seams to ¼"; press B to the right side to complete one A-B unit. Repeat for 51 units.

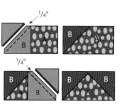

Figure 1

3. Repeat step 2 with C and D pieces to complete one C-D unit referring to Figure 2; repeat for 54 C-D units.

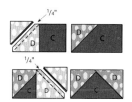

Figure 2

4. Select 10 each A-B and C-D units; join units starting with an A-B unit and alternating with C-D units to make a 20-unit strip for Row 1; press seams toward A and C pieces.

5. Repeat step 4 to make a 19-unit strip for Row 2 with nine A-B units and 10 C-D units referring to the Placement Diagram for positioning of first unit.

6. Repeat step 4 to make an 18-unit strip for Row 3 with nine each A-B and C-D units.

7. Repeat step 4 to make a 17-unit strip for Row 4 with eight A-B and nine C-D units.

8. Repeat step 4 to make a 16-unit strip for Row 5 with eight each A-B and C-D units.

9. Repeat step 4 to make a 15-unit strip for Row 6 with seven A-B and eight C-D units.

10. Sew E to the C bottom end of each row referring to the Placement Diagram; press seams toward E.

11. Sew an F square to the E end of Rows 2–6, again referring to the Placement Diagram; press seams toward F.

12. Join the rows in numerical order referring to the Placement Diagram; press seams in one direction.

13. Sew G to the Row 1 side and H to the Row 6 side of the pieced top; press seams toward G and H.

14. Sew I to the top of the pieced center to complete the top; press seam toward I.

Finishing the Quilt

1. Lay the batting on a flat surface; place the backing piece right side up on the batting. Place the stitched top right sides together with the backing; pin layers together to keep flat.

2. Stitch all around outside edges using a ¼" seam allowance, leaving an 8" opening on one side.

3. Clip corners and trim backing and batting even with edges of quilt top.

4. Turn right side out through opening; press edges flat and opening edges inside ¼"; hand-stitch opening closed.

5. Machine- or hand-quilt as desired.

6. Cut a 3½" by fabric width strip purple solid for the hanging sleeve. Turn under each end ¼" and ¼" again; stitch to hem.

7. Fold and stitch strip with right sides together along length to make a tube. Turn the tube right side out; press with seam at the bottom edge.

8. Hand-stitch each edge of the hanging sleeve to the top edge of the backing, being careful not to catch the right side of the quilt in the stitching.

9. Cut one 12" length and five 6" lengths beaded trim. Hand-stitch the beaded trim pieces to the bottom wrong-side edge of each section, referring to the Placement Diagram for positioning. ■

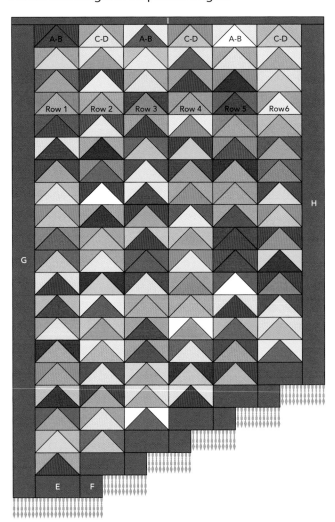

The Romance of Camelot
Placement Diagram
42" x 64"

Deck the Halls

Add a touch of quilted elegance to your holidays. Here's five projects that will add a festive ambience to your home and show off your quilting skills.

Christmas Hospitality Runner

Creative combinations of half-square triangles results in a striking holiday bed runner.

DESIGNED & QUILTED BY WENDY SHEPPARD

PROJECT SPECIFICATIONS

Skill Level: Confident Beginner
Runner Size: 65⅝" x 25⅞"
Block Size: 12" x 12"
Number of Blocks: 3

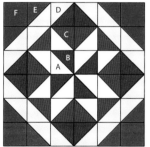

Noel Star 1
12" x 12" Block
Make 2

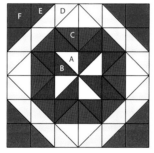

Noel Star 2
12" x 12" Block
Make 1

MATERIALS

¼ yard white-with-black print
¼ yard black print
½ yard black-with-white print
⅜ yard red print
½ yard red tonal
⅝ yard black poinsettia print
1¼ yards white-with-red print
Backing 73" x 34"
Batting 73" x 34"
Neutral-color all-purpose thread
Quilting thread
Basic sewing tools and supplies

Cutting

1. Cut two 2⅞" by fabric width strips white-with-black print; subcut strips into 18 (2⅞") squares. Cut each square in half on one diagonal to make 36 A triangles.

2. Cut two 2⅞" by fabric width strips black print; subcut strips into 18 (2⅞") squares. Cut each square in half on one diagonal to make 36 C triangles.

3. Cut one 12½" by fabric width strip black-with-white print; subcut strip into 12 (2½") G rectangles.

4. Cut two 2⅞" by fabric width strips red print; subcut strips into 16 (2⅞") squares. Cut each square in half on one diagonal to make 32 E triangles.

5. Cut one 2½" by fabric width strip red print; subcut strip into 14 (2½) F squares.

6. Cut two 2⅞" by fabric width strips red tonal; subcut strips into 18 (2⅞") squares. Cut each square in half on one diagonal to make 36 B triangles.

7. Cut three 1½" by fabric width J strips red tonal.

8. Cut two 1½" x 22⅜" K strips red tonal.

9. Cut two 2½" x 22⅜" L strips black poinsettia print.

10. Cut four 2½" by fabric width M strips black poinsettia print.

11. Cut three 2⅞" by fabric width strips white-with-red print; subcut strips into 30 (2⅞") squares. Cut each square in half on one diagonal to make 60 D triangles.

12. Cut one 18¼" by fabric width strip white-with-red print; subcut strip into one 18¼" square and two 9⅜" squares. Cut the 18¼" square on both diagonals to make four I triangles. Cut the 9⅜" squares in half on one diagonal to make four H triangles.

13. Cut five 2¼" by fabric width strips white-with-red print for binding.

Completing the Blocks

1. *Note:* *Refer to Figure 1 for Steps 1–4 for making stitched units.* Sew A to B along the diagonal to make an A-B unit as shown in Figure 1; press seam toward B. Repeat to make a total of 12 A-B units. Repeat with C and D to make 12 C-D units; press seams toward C.

Figure 1

2. Repeat step 1 with A and C, and B and D to make 16 each A-C and B-D units; press seams toward B and C.

3. Repeat step 1 with B and C, and A and D to make eight each B-C and A-D units; press seams toward B and D.

4. Repeat step 1 with D and E to make 24 D-E units; press seams toward E.

5. To make one Noel Star 1 block, arrange and join four each A-B and C-D units and eight each A-C, B-D and D-E units with four F squares in six rows of six units each, referring to Figure 2 for positioning of units and F; press seams in adjoining rows in opposite directions.

Figure 2

6. Join the rows as arranged in Figure 2 and referring to the block drawing to complete one Noel Star 1 block; press seams in one direction.

7. Repeat steps 5 and 6 to complete a second Noel Star 1 block.

8. To make the Noel Star 2 block, arrange and join four each A-B and C-D units, and eight each B-C, A-D and D-E units with four F squares in six rows of six units each, referring to Figure 3 for positioning of units with F; press seams in adjoining rows in opposite directions.

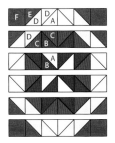

Figure 3

9. Join the rows as arranged in Figure 3 and referring to the block drawing to complete the Noel Star 2 block; press seams in one direction.

Completing the Runner

1. Arrange and join the Noel Star 2 block and the Noel Star 1 blocks with the F squares and G sashing strips, and the E, H and I triangles in diagonal rows referring to Figure 4; press seams toward the G sashing strips.

Figure 4

2. Join the rows, adding H to opposite corners to complete the runner center; press seams toward the G sashing rows.

3. Join three J strips on short ends to make one long strip; press seams open. Subcut strip into two 60⅛" J strips.

4. Sew a J strip to opposite long sides and K strips to the short ends of the runner center; press seams toward J and K strips.

5. Sew an L strip to opposite short ends of the runner center; press seams toward L strips.

6. Join the four M strips on short ends to make one long strip; press seams open. Subcut strip into two 66⅛" M strips.

7. Sew an M strip to opposite long sides to complete the pieced runner; press seams toward M strips.

8. Layer, quilt and bind referring to Finishing Your Quilt on page 160. ■

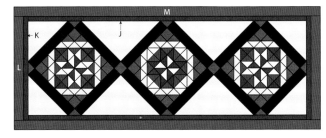

Christmas Hospitality Runner
Placement Diagram 65⅝" x 25⅞"

Flourish Christmas Table Runner

Flaunt your quilting skills on your holiday table. Set the perfect table.

DESIGN BY CAROLYN S. VAGTS FOR THE VILLAGE PATTERN CO.

PROJECT SPECIFICATIONS

Skill Level: Beginner
Runner Size: 44" x 20"
Block Size: 4" x 4"
Number of Blocks: 27

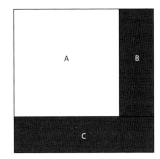

Flourish
4" x 4" Block
Make 27

MATERIALS

¼ yard red tonal
⅜ yard coordinating stripe
⅜ yard red with gold stars
½ yard cream with gold stars
1⅝ yards poinsettia floral
Batting 52" x 28"
Coordinating all-purpose thread
Basic sewing tools and supplies

Cutting

1. Cut a 28" x 52" backing rectangle along the length of the poinsettia floral.

2. Cut two 3½" x 44½" G strips along the length of the poinsettia floral.

3. Cut two 3½" x 14½" F strips from the remainder of the poinsettia floral.

4. Cut three 3½" by fabric width A strips cream with gold stars.

5. Cut four 2½" by fabric width strips coordinating stripe for binding.

6. Cut three 1½" by fabric width B strips red with gold stars.

7. Cut one 4½" by fabric width strip red with gold stars; subcut strip into 27 (1½") C rectangles.

8. Cut three 1½" by fabric width strips red tonal; subcut one strip into two 12½" D strips. Trim the remaining strips to make two 38½" E strips.

Completing the Blocks

1. Sew a B strip to an A strip with right sides together along length to make an A-B strip set; press seam toward the B strip. Repeat to make a total of three A-B strip sets.

2. Subcut the A-B strip sets into 27 (3½") A-B units as shown in Figure 1.

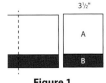

Figure 1

3. Sew a C rectangle to the bottom of an A-B unit to complete one Flourish block as shown in Figure 2; press seam toward C.

Figure 2

2. Matching the A sides, join four block pairs; add one single block to the end to complete an X row referring to Figure 4. Press all seams toward the single block. Repeat to make a second X row.

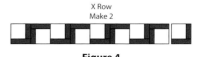

Figure 4

3. Repeat step 2 except sew the single block to the opposite end of the block strip to make a Y row as shown in Figure 5; press all seams toward the single block.

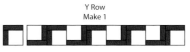

Figure 5

4. Sew an X row to opposite sides of the Y row, matching seams, to complete the pieced center referring to Figure 6; press seams in one direction.

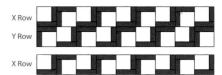

Figure 6

5. Referring to the Placement Diagram, sew a D strip to each short end of the pieced center; press seams toward D strips.

6. Sew an E strip to opposite long sides of the pieced center; press seams toward E strips.

7. Sew F strips to the short ends and G strips to opposite long sides of the pieced center to complete the runner, again referring to the Placement Diagram; press seams toward F and G strips.

8. Layer, quilt and bind the runner referring to Finishing Your Quilt on page 160. ■

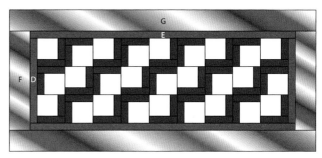

Flourish Christmas Table Runner
Placement Diagram 44" x 20"

4. Repeat step 3 to make a total of 27 Flourish blocks.

Completing the Runner

1. Matching the B sides, join two Flourish blocks to make a block pair referring to Figure 3. Repeat to make a total of 12 block pairs.

Figure 3

Angels Among Us

Circle your tree with angels for the perfect finishing touch.

DESIGN BY CHRIS MALONE

PROJECT SPECIFICATIONS

Skill Level: Confident Beginner
Tree Skirt Size: 40" diameter (not including prairie points)

MATERIALS

1 (10" x 10") scrap each 4 green prints
1 fat quarter each pink solid, gold tonal and white tonal
¼ yard each 5 assorted red, green and white prints
1⅜ yards red snowflake print
1⅜ yards red dot
Batting 44" x 44"
Thread to match fabrics
3 yards tan loopy yarn
2 yards 1"-wide red grosgrain ribbon
Double-sheet newspaper at least 44" square, pencil and 24" string
1 yard 18"-wide fusible web
Nonstick pressing sheet
16 (⅛") black buttons
8 (⅝") gold star buttons
Cosmetic powder blush and cotton-tip swab
Walking foot for sewing machine (optional)
Basic sewing tools and supplies

Cutting

1. Fold the newspaper in quarters.

2. Tie one end of the string to the pencil and measure 20½" from the tied end.

3. Hold the 20½" point of the string at the folded corner of the paper. Holding the pencil perpendicular to the paper, mark a quarter-circle on the paper as shown in Figure 1.

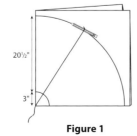

Figure 1

4. Repeat step 3 with the string only 3" long to mark an inner quarter-circle, again referring to Figure 1.

5. Cut out the paper pattern on the marked lines. Unfold flat and cut paper pattern along one fold line to make the tree-skirt pattern as shown in Figure 2.

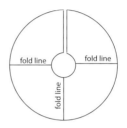

Figure 2

6. Using the pattern, cut one tree skirt from red dot for the tree-skirt top and one from red snowflake print for the tree-skirt backing.

7. Cut a 4½" by fabric width strip from each of the assorted ¼-yard fabrics; subcut each strip into 4½" squares to cut a total of 39 assorted squares.

Preparing & Completing the Appliqué

1. Trace appliqué shapes given onto the paper side of the fusible web referring to patterns for number to cut and leaving ½" between shapes when tracing.

2. Cut out shapes, leaving a margin around each one.

3. Fuse shapes to the wrong side of fabrics as directed on each piece for color; cut out shapes on traced lines. Remove paper backing; set aside.

4. Stitch a scant ¼" from the cut edge of the center circle of the tree-skirt top.

5. Select pieces for one angel motif. Arrange these pieces on the nonstick pressing sheet in numerical order referring to the appliqué motif. ***Note:*** *You may place a copy of the angel motif under the pressing sheet to be used as a guide, if desired.* When satisfied with positioning, fuse shapes in place. Repeat to make a total of eight angel motifs.

6. Fuse an angel motif about 5" from an opening edge and 3" from the outer edge of the tree-skirt top as shown in Figure 3.

Figure 3

7. Arrange and fuse the remaining seven angel motifs around the tree skirt with approximately 5" between the hand of one angel and the foot of the next angel, again referring to Figure 3.

8. Fuse the star shapes ³⁄₈" below the hand of each angel motif referring to Figure 4.

Figure 4

9. Using thread to match fabrics, machine blanket-stitch around each appliqué shape.

Completing the Tree Skirt

1. Fold a 4½" square in half on one diagonal. Fold in half again to form a prairie point referring to Figure 5; press flat.

Figure 5

2. Repeat step 1 to make a total of 39 assorted prairie points.

3. Pin the raw edge of the prairie points to the curved bottom edge of the appliquéd tree-skirt top, sliding one point into the fold of the next point, overlapping about 1" as shown in Figure 6. Machine-baste to secure.

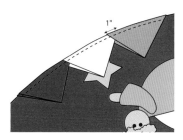

Figure 6

4. Cut the grosgrain ribbon into four 18" lengths.

5. Pin and baste one end of a grosgrain ribbon piece ³⁄₈" down from the center circle along the opening as shown in Figure 7.

Figure 7

6. Pin and baste one end of a second grosgrain ribbon piece 9" down from the first ribbon along the same opening, again referring to Figure 7.

7. Repeat steps 5 and 6 on the opposite opening side.

8. Place the batting square on a flat surface. Layer the tree-skirt backing right side up on the batting; place the appliquéd tree-skirt top right side down on the backing, matching raw edges. Pin the layers together along tree-skirt edges.

9. Stitch a ¼" seam allowance all around all edges, leaving an opening between the ribbons on one side for turning; clip curves and corners. Trim batting close to stitching.

10. Turn right side out through the opening; fold opening seam allowance to the inside and hand-stitch closed.

11. Topstitch ¼" from all edges.

12. Quilt as desired. **Note:** *The sample has stitching around each angel and star using red thread. A double line of gold stitching connects the star and hand. A star is quilted in red above and between the angels.*

13. Sew two ⅛" black buttons to each angel face for eyes as indicated on pattern.

14. Using the cotton-tip swab, apply blush to angel cheeks.

15. To make angel's hair, cut the yarn into eight 13½" lengths. Wrap one length around three fingers to make a bundle; remove from fingers as a bundle and secure with a doubled length of gold thread referring to Figure 8.

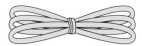

Figure 8

16. With the gold thread, sew a ⅝" gold star button to the center of the hair bundle. Then sew hair and button to top of angel's head. Pull pieces apart to make loopy curls. Repeat for all angels referring to the Placement Diagram to finish. ■

Angels Among Us
Placement Diagram 40" diameter (not including prairie points)

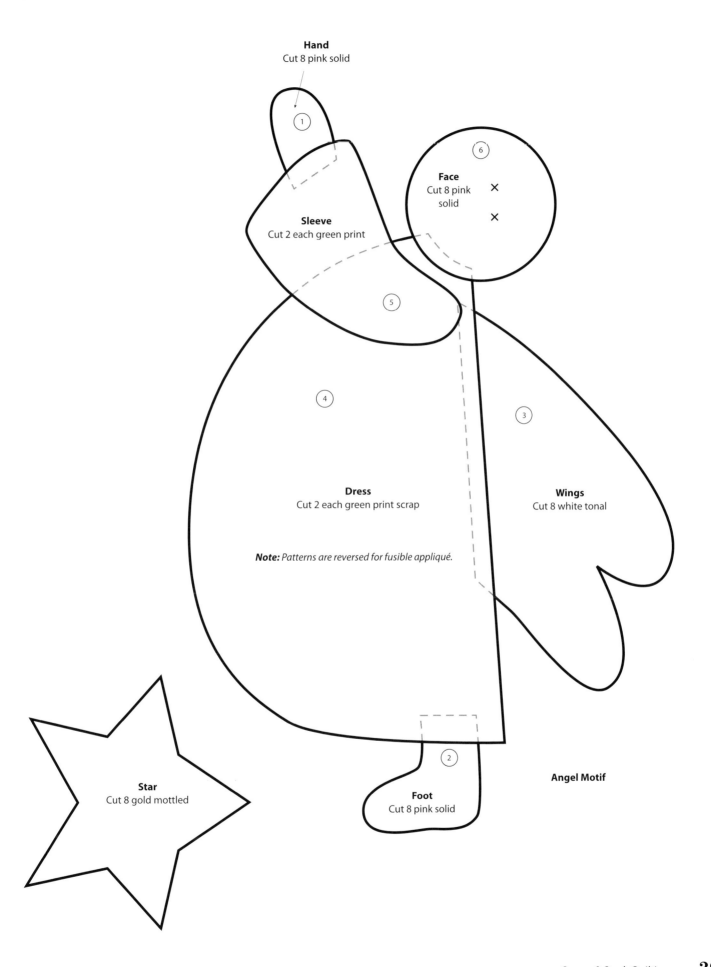

Hand
Cut 8 pink solid

1

Face
Cut 8 pink solid

6

Sleeve
Cut 2 each green print

5

4

Dress
Cut 2 each green print scrap

3

Wings
Cut 8 white tonal

Note: Patterns are reversed for fusible appliqué.

Angel Motif

2

Star
Cut 8 gold mottled

Foot
Cut 8 pink solid

Holiday Joy

Spread some joy this holiday season. A creative wall hanging on a door sends a cheerful message.

DESIGN BY CAROLYN S. VAGTS FOR THE VILLAGE PATTERN CO.

PROJECT SPECIFICATIONS

Skill Level: Confident Beginner
Wall Hanging Size: 12" x 52" including cord, tassel and hanger

MATERIALS

2 (8") squares green batik
¼ yard green tonal
⅓ yard red mottled
1⅓ yards cream tonal
3 (14") squares batting
All-purpose thread to match fabrics
Quilting thread
3 (⅜") green buttons
3 (⅝") red buttons
½ yard 18"-wide fusible web
1 (3") red tassel
4 yards red drapery twisted cord
3 (11") ⅜"-diameter wooden dowels
Basic sewing tools and supplies

Cutting

1. Cut four 1¼" by fabric width strips green tonal; subcut strips into 12 (13") B strips.

2. Cut one 12½" by fabric width strip cream tonal; subcut strip into three 12½" A squares.

3. Cut one 14" by fabric width strip cream tonal; subcut strip into three 14" backing squares.

4. Cut one 2½" x 42" strip cream tonal; set aside.

5. Cut one 2" by fabric width strip cream tonal; subcut strip into three 12" C strips for dowel sleeves.

6. Cut four 2¼" by fabric width strips cream tonal for binding.

Completing the Panels

1. Trace the J, O and Y letter patterns onto the paper side of the fusible web, leaving ½" between letters; cut out letters, leaving a margin around each one.

2. Fuse letters to the wrong side of the red mottled; cut out on traced lines. Remove paper backing.

3. Fold each A square in half vertically and horizontally, and crease to mark the centers.

4. Center and fuse a letter to each A square.

5. Using a close blanket stitch and red thread to match fabric, machine-stitch around the inside and outside edges of each letter.

6. Sandwich a 14" batting square between a 14" backing square and a fused A square; pin or baste layers together to hold. Quilt as desired by hand or machine. When quilting is complete, remove pins or basting, and trim batting and backing edges even with the fused A square.

7. Repeat step 6 with remaining fused A squares.

8. Fold each B strip with wrong sides together along length; press.

9. Using a ⅛" seam allowance, stitch one folded B strip to opposite sides of one quilted A square matching raw edges of B with raw edges of A as shown in Figure 1. Trim B even with A square.

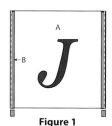

Figure 1

10. Stitch a second set of folded B strips to the remaining sides of A, folding each end at an angle to form a miter before stitching as shown in Figure 2.

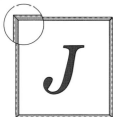

Figure 2

11. Repeat steps 9 and 10 on the remaining quilted A squares.

Completing the Hanging

1. Fold the 2½" x 42" strip cream tonal in half along length with right sides together and sew along the long raw edge to make a tube; turn right side out with a safety pin. Press with seam centered on one side. Subcut tube into 12 (2") lengths as shown in Figure 3. Fold each length in half with the seam on the inside to make a loop, again referring to Figure 3; machine-baste the raw edges together.

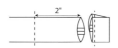

Figure 3

2. Pin and baste a loop 1" down from each top corner and 1" up from each bottom corner on the wrong side of each quilted A square as shown in Figure 4.

Figure 4

3. Fold each short end of each C strip under ¼" and ¼" again and stitch to hem.

4. Fold each C strip in half with wrong sides together along length; center and pin one strip to the top back side of each quilted A

square, right side out with raw edges matching as shown in Figure 5; baste in place to hold and to make the dowel sleeves.

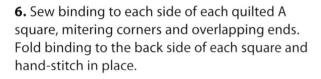

Figure 5

5. Join the binding strips on short ends to make one long strip. Fold the strip in half along length with wrong sides together; press.

6. Sew binding to each side of each quilted A square, mitering corners and overlapping ends. Fold binding to the back side of each square and hand-stitch in place.

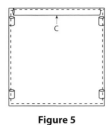

Holiday Joy
Placement Diagram 12" x 52",
including cord, tassel and hanger

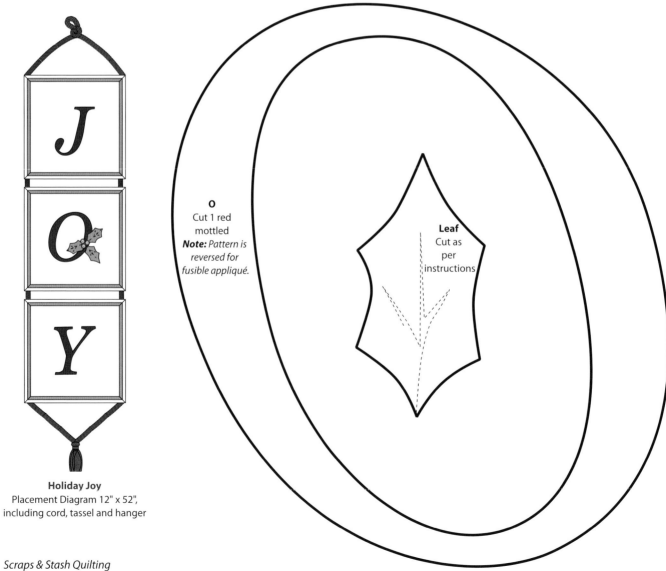

O
Cut 1 red
mottled
*Note: Pattern is
reversed for
fusible appliqué.*

Leaf
Cut as
per
instructions

7. Hand-stitch the long bottom edge of each dowel sleeve in place on the back side of each quilted A square.

8. Using the fusible web, fuse the two 8" squares green batik with wrong sides together.

9. Trace three leaf shapes onto one side of the fused layers; trace and cut out.

10. Pin the three leaves on the O letter referring to the Placement Diagram for positioning; machine-stitch each leaf in place around outer edge and on inner lines as marked on pattern using thread to match leaf fabric.

11. Layer a green button on a red button and sew the layered buttons on the inside tip of a leaf referring to the Placement Diagram for positioning. Repeat with the remaining buttons.

12. Thread the drapery cord through the 12 loops starting at one side of the bottom letter Y, moving up through the O and J and then down the other side, through the J, then O and finally Y, leaving enough extra for 1" to show between panels and room at the top to tie a knot to make a hanging loop tacking in place at side loops. Bring the two bottom ends together and tie the tassel at the bottom center to finish. ***Note:*** *Certain drapery cords may need to be stitched together at a point where they will not show. Some cord will unravel. If the cord you choose is one that unravels, attach it so that the seam is behind one of the blocks out of sight.*

13. Insert an 11" wooden dowel into each of the dowel sleeves to hang. ***Note:*** *The dowels add stability.* ■

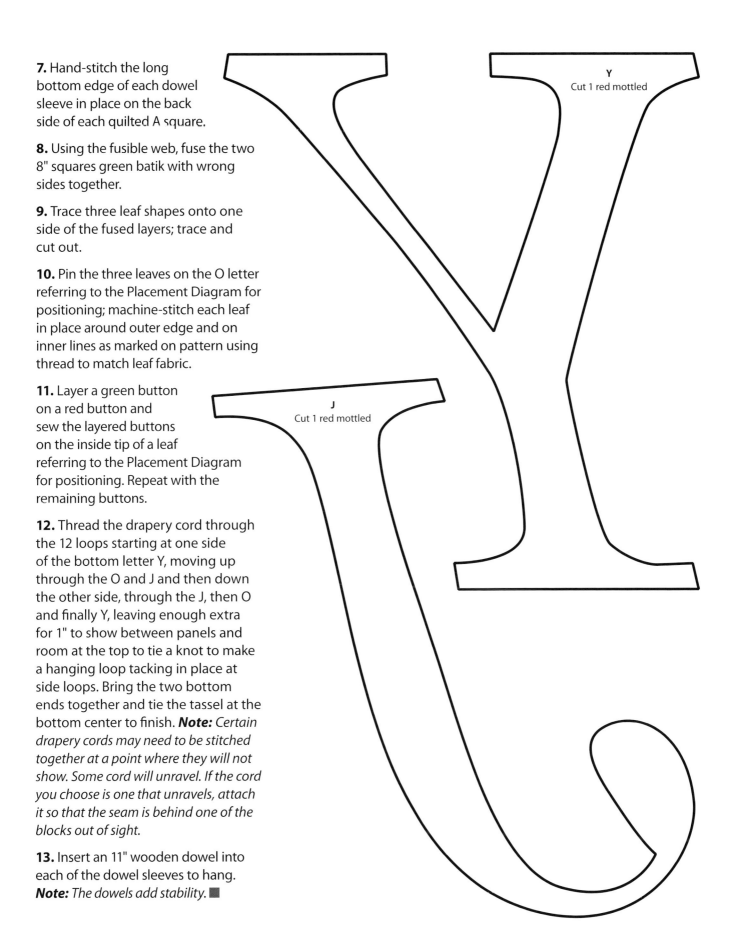

Y
Cut 1 red mottled

J
Cut 1 red mottled

Old St. Nick

"His eyes—how they twinkled! His dimples how merry!
His cheeks were like roses, his nose like a cherry!"
            —*From* Twas the Night Before Christmas *by Clement Clarke Moore*

DESIGN BY CHRIS MALONE

PROJECT SPECIFICATIONS

Skill Level: Confident Beginner
Wall Hanging Size: 12" x 24"

MATERIALS

Scraps red and light pink solids, and cream tonal
1 fat quarter green print
⅓ yard black holly print
⅓ yard white mini dot
Backing 16½" x 12½"
Batting 16½" x 12½"
Scrap thin batting 12" x 15" for beard, mustache and
    hat trim
All-purpose thread to match fabrics
Quilting thread
⅜"-diameter gold jingle bell
Powdered blush and cotton-tip swab
2 (¾") plastic rings or prepared hanging sleeve
2 (⁹⁄₁₆") black buttons
1 (¾") any-color shank button
Basic sewing tools and supplies

Cutting

1. Cut one 11½" x 7½" A rectangle green print.

2. Cut two 3" by fabric width strips black holly print; subcut strips into two 11½" B strips and two 12½" C strips.

Prepare & Appliqué Santa Motif

1. Prepare templates for face and hat shapes using patterns provided; cut the hat and face pieces as directed on patterns, adding ¼" seam allowance all around for hand appliqué. Do not add seam allowance to the bottom edge of the hat.

2. Center and pin the face shape to A 4" from the top edge as shown in Figure 1; hand-stitch in place with thread to match pink fabric.

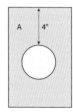

Figure 1

3. Turn under edges of hat shape ¼" except along bottom edge; pin hat to A, overlapping face referring to the pattern for positioning; hand-stitch in place with thread to match red fabric.

4. Fold cream tonal fabric in half with right sides together, trace the hat-trim pattern onto one side of the folded cream tonal. With traced pattern side on top, pin the folded fabric to the scrap of thin batting. Sew all around on the traced lines as shown in Figure 2.

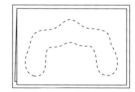

Figure 2

5. Cut out ⅛" from stitched line; trim batting close to seam and clip curves. Cut a slash through one layer of fabric only, where indicated on pattern. Turn right side out through the slash; press edges flat.

6. Position the hat-trim piece on the bottom of the hat, covering the raw edges and the top of the face referring to the pattern; hand-stitch in place using thread to match cream fabric.

7. Fold the white mini dot fabric in half with right sides together. Trace the beard, mustache and one reversed mustache pieces onto one side of the folded white mini dot. With traced pattern side on top, pin folded fabric to a scrap of thin batting as shown in Figure 3.

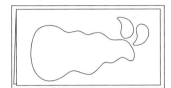

Figure 3

8. Sew all around each shape on the traced lines; cut out shapes ⅛" from seam. Trim batting close to the seam and clip curves. Cut a slash through one layer of fabric only, where indicated on patterns. Turn right side out through the slash; press edges flat.

9. Transfer the quilting design to the beard and mustache pieces using a water-erasable marker or pencil. Quilt by hand or machine on the marked lines. Remove any marks and set these pieces aside.

Completing the Quilt

1. Sew a B strip to opposite long sides and C strips to the top and bottom of A; press seams toward B and C strips.

2. Layer the backing piece right side up on the batting rectangle; place the appliquéd top right side against the backing and pin to secure. Stitch all around, leaving a 5" opening along the bottom edge.

3. Trim the batting close to the seam, clip corners and turn right side out through the opening; press edges flat.

4. Turn the seam allowance in the opening to the inside; hand-stitch opening closed.

5. Quilt as desired by hand or machine.

6. When quilting is complete, position and pin the beard and mustache pieces on the face referring to the Placement Diagram for positioning; using thread to match fabrics, hand-stitch the beard edges to the quilt and the bottom edge of the mustache pieces to the beard.

Old St. Nick
Placement Diagram 12" x 24"

7. Cut a 1¾" circle from a scrap of light pink solid using the nose pattern given; finger-press ⅛" under all around and baste to hold using a knotted thread, leaving the thread tails when finished. Place the shank button in the center of the fabric circle and pull on the thread tails to gather the fabric over the button and around the shank as shown in Figure 4; pull the thread tight and knot to make the nose. **Note:** *A circle of batting may be glued to the top of the button before covering, if desired.*

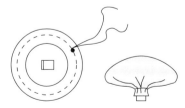

Figure 4

8. Use a cotton tip swab to apply a light circle of blush to each cheek area and to the center of the nose.

9. Sew the button nose to the face above the mustache as marked on pattern.

10. Sew the black buttons to the face for eyes as marked on pattern.

11. Sew the bell to the tip of the hat.

12. Sew the plastic rings to the upper back corners of the wall quilt for hanger or attach prepared hanging sleeve. ■

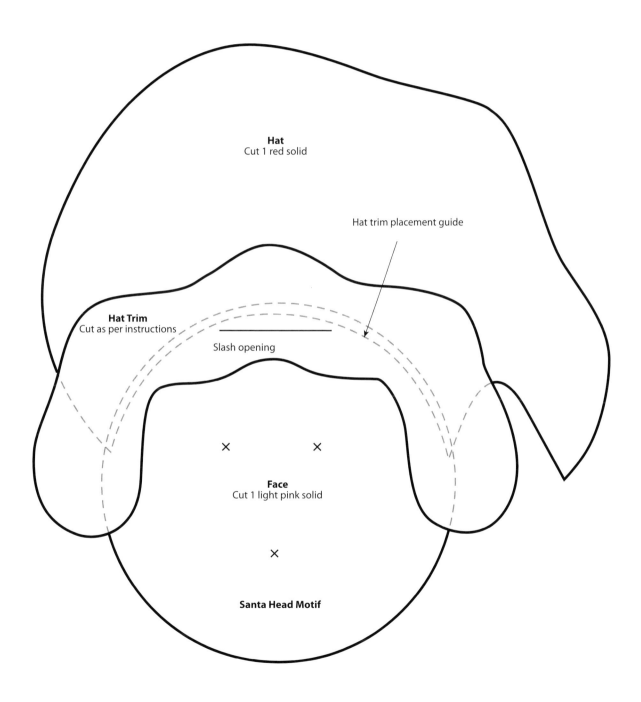

Hat
Cut 1 red solid

Hat trim placement guide

Hat Trim
Cut as per instructions

Slash opening

Face
Cut 1 light pink solid

Santa Head Motif

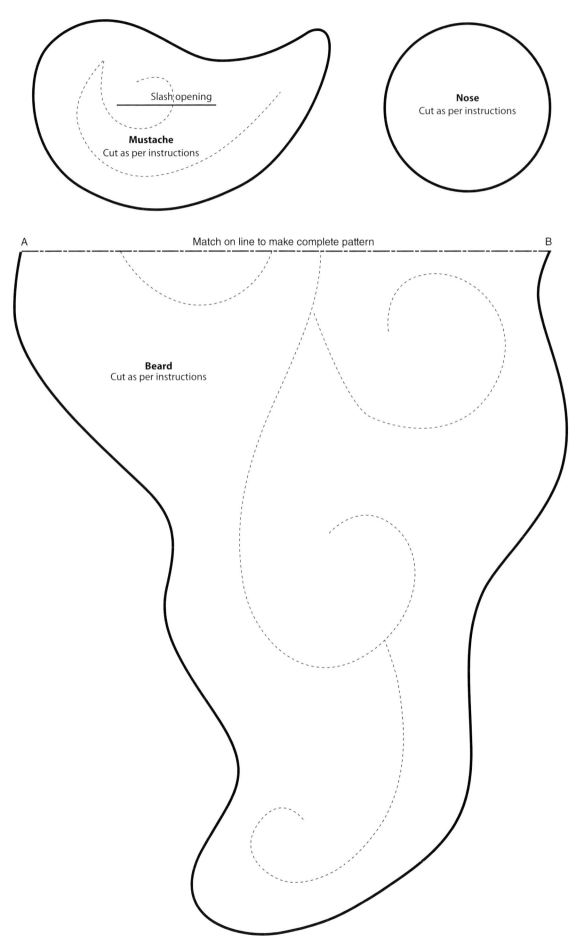

Slash opening

Mustache
Cut as per instructions

Nose
Cut as per instructions

A   Match on line to make complete pattern   B

Beard
Cut as per instructions

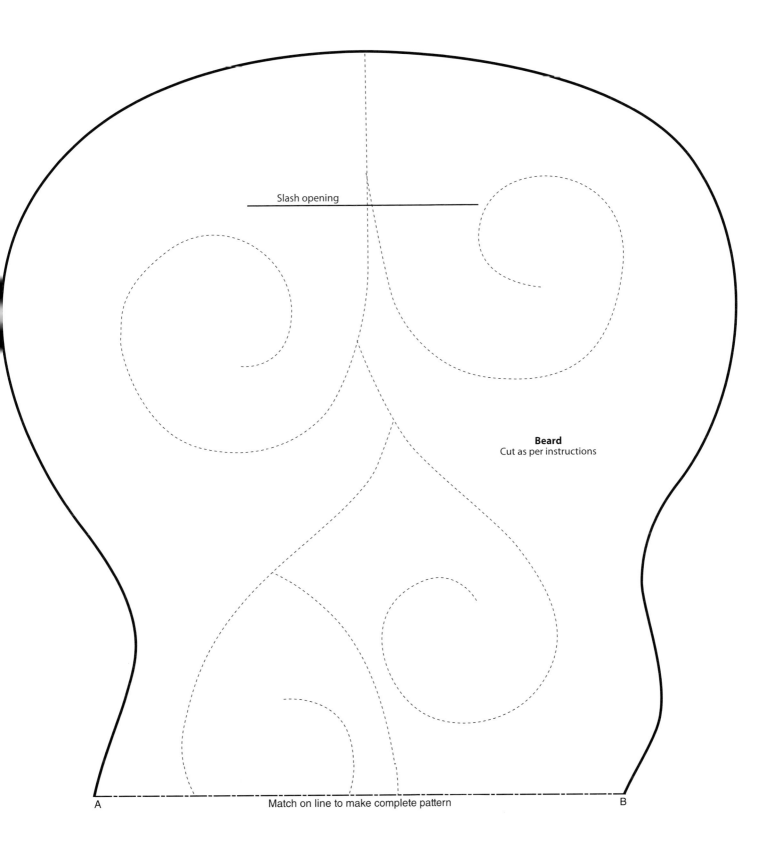

Slash opening

Beard
Cut as per instructions

A   Match on line to make complete pattern   B

Scrappy Treasures

Timeless designs in a range of sizes perfect for using your scraps and stash. Turn your scrap basket into fabulous quilts.

Bull's-Eye

How many games at the fair require tossing a dart or ball to hit the bull's-eye to win a prize? This quilt is a definite winner!

DESIGN BY JEAN ANN WRIGHT
QUILTED BY SHANNON BAKER

PROJECT SPECIFICATIONS

Skill Level: Confident Beginner
Quilt Size: 58" x 66"
Block Size: 8" x 8"
Number of Blocks: 30

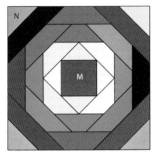

Pineapple
8" x 8" Block
Make 30

MATERIALS

1 fat eighth (or scraps) 10 different each:
    red prints
    gold prints
    teal prints
    white-with-black prints
    black-with-white prints
⅞ yard black mini dot
1¾ yards large focus print
Backing 66" x 74"
Batting 66" x 74"
Thread
Pineapple Tool™ by Gyleen (optional)
Basic sewing tools and supplies

PROJECT NOTES

You will need to use contrasting thread in the bobbin when sewing seams because you must be able to see the bobbin thread when trimming with the Pineapple Tool™, or any other trimming ruler.

You may use another type of square ruler with a ¼" grid, but the Pineapple Tool takes the guesswork out of watching all the lines.

Although this quilt uses a variety of scraps, they are planned color families in red, black, white, gold and teal with planned color placement.

If you want to duplicate this quilt, refer to the Placement Diagram to make blocks in specific color versions. If you prefer a more unplanned, scrappy look, you might choose a variety of scraps with just two colors for the N corner triangles. This will make a pattern when the triangles meet as rows are joined as shown in Figure 2 on page 52. These colors could match border fabrics, bringing those fabrics into the quilt center, again referring to Figure 2.

Cutting

1. From each red, gold and teal print, cut one 3" x 21" strip; subcut strip into two 3" squares and one 2½" M square. Subcut each 3" square in half on one diagonal to make a total of 40 N triangles.

2. Cut all remaining red, gold and teal prints into 1½" x 21" strips.

3. Cut 1½" x 21" strips from all white-with-black and black-with-white prints

4. Cut five 1½" by fabric width black mini dot O/P strips.

5. Cut seven 2¼" by fabric width black mini dot strips for binding.

6. Cut two 8½" x 50½" Q strips along length of large focus print.

7. Cut two 8½" x 58½" R strips along length of large focus print.

Color Planning

1. Refer to Figure 1 for color planning beginning the blocks with M squares in red, yellow or teal and referring to the round colors for each lettered block (see Figure 5 on page 54), adding N corner triangles in colors shown for each version of the blocks referring to Figure 2.

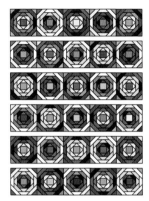

Figure 1

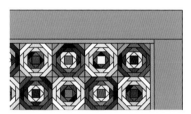

Figure 2

Completing the Blocks

1. Select one red M square, four gold N triangles, and eight different 1½"-wide strips each black-with-white, teal and white-with-black prints. ***Note:*** *The strips may be trimmed to 1" longer than the side to which they will be sewn, if you prefer to work with shorter strips as you stitch.*

2. Sew a white-with-black print strip to each side of the M square with right sides together using either a scant or perfect ¼" seam allowance; trim the strips, leaving ½" extending beyond the M square on each end. Press each seam toward the strip as you sew in place (Photo 1).

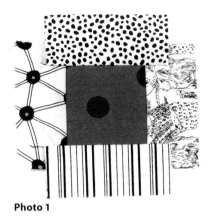

Photo 1

3. Place the Pineapple Tool on the wrong side of the stitched unit so that the cut edge of the center square is against the diagonal lines and the centerline of the tool passes through the seam intersection as shown in Figure 3.

Figure 3

4. Trim excess even with edges of the tool using a rotary cutter.

5. Repeat step 4 on each corner to complete round 1 as shown in Photo 2. ***Note:*** *Round 1 is the only one that uses the diagonal lines on the pineapple tool.*

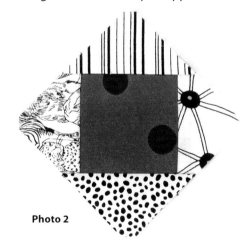

Photo 2

6. Add a second round of white-with-black print strips around the trimmed unit as in step 2 and Photo 3.

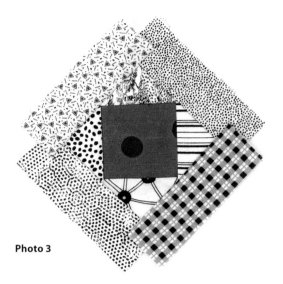

Photo 3

7. Place the tool on the wrong side of the stitched unit, aligning the 1" line on the tool with the raw edge of the stitched seam between the M center and the first round and trim to complete round 2 as shown in Photo 4 and Figure 4.

Figure 4

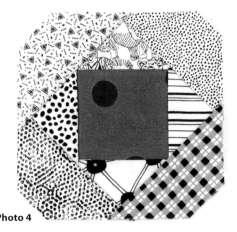

Photo 4

8. Continue to add 1½"-wide strips around the M center, trimming after each round and adding two rounds each of teal and black-with-white prints to complete six rounds.

9. Center and sew an N triangle to each corner of the stitched unit as shown in Figure 5; press seam toward N.

Figure 5

10. Trim excess N and square up the finished block to 8½" x 8½" as shown in Photos 5 and 6.

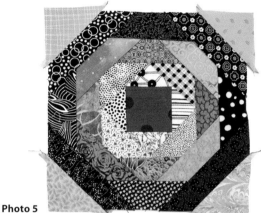

Photo 5

Photo 6

11. Repeat steps 1–10 to complete a total of two each E, F, H, J, K and L, and three each A, B, C, D, G and I referring to Figure 6 for color selection and placement.

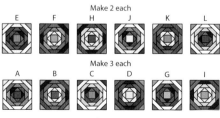

Figure 6

Completing the Quilt

1. Select and join blocks in six rows of five blocks each referring to Figure 7 for block placement by letter; press seams in adjoining rows in opposite directions. **Note:** *Handle and press the blocks carefully. The trimmed edges are bias and will stretch easily.*

B	C	D	E	F
G	B	C	H	E
I	G	B	J	H
A	I	G	K	J
D	A	I	L	K
C	D	A	F	L

Figure 7

2. Join the rows as stitched to complete the pieced center; press seams in one direction.

3. Join the O/P strips on short ends to make one long strip; press seams open. Subcut strip into two 48½" O strips and two 42½" P strips.

4. Sew an O strip to opposite long sides and P strips to the top and bottom of the pieced center; press seams toward O and P strips.

5. Sew a Q strip to opposite long sides and R strips to the top and bottom of the pieced center; press seams toward Q and R strips.

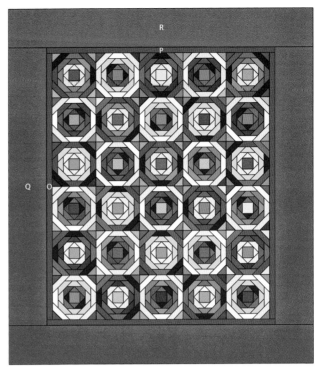

Bull's-Eye
Placement Diagram 58" x 66"

6. Layer, quilt and bind referring to Finishing Your Quilt on page 160. ■

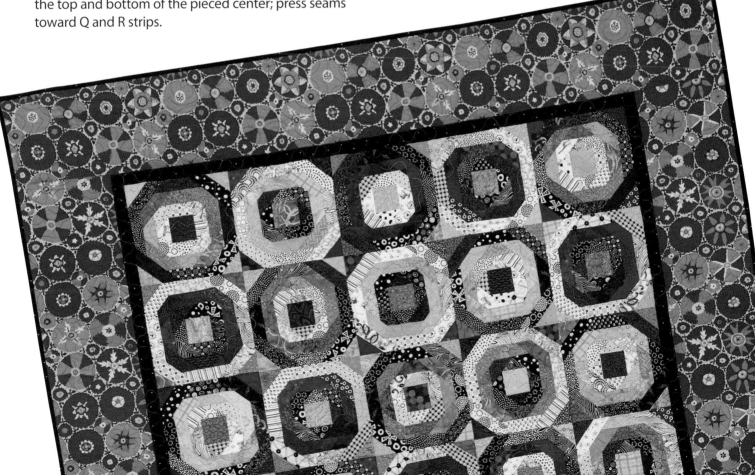

Piece-Full Days

If you have lots of scraps and leftover fabric strips, this is the quilt for you. The more variety, the better it will look. Clean out your scrap basket and create a treasure at the same time.

DESIGN BY RUTH ANN SHEFFIELD

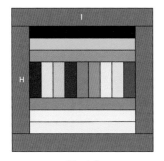

Block 1
12" x 12" Block
Make 5

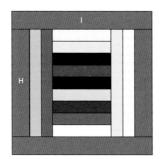

Block 2
12" x 12" Block
Make 5

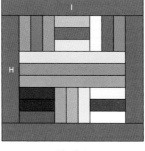

Block 3
12" x 12" Block
Make 5

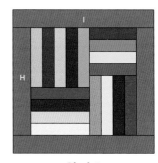

Block 4
12" x 12" Block
Make 5

PROJECT SPECIFICATIONS

Skill Level: Intermediate
Quilt Size: 64" x 78"
Block Size: 12" x 12"
Number of Blocks: 20

MATERIALS

66 (1½" x 42") precut or scrap strips
294 (2⅞") squares assorted scraps
Assorted 1¾"-wide strips total 275" for border 1
Assorted 2¼"-wide strips to total 285" for border 2
2⅓ yards black solid
Backing 72" x 86"
Batting 72" x 86"
Thread
Basic sewing tools and supplies

Cutting

1. Cut and piece 1¾"-wide border 1 strips to make two each 1¾" x 72½" L and 1¾" x 61" M border strips.

2. Cut and piece 2¼"-wide border 2 strips to make two each 2¼" x 75" N and 1¾" x 64½" O border strips.

3. Cut two 9½" by fabric width black solid strips; subcut into 40 (2" x 9½") H strips.

4. Cut two 12½" by fabric width black solid strips; subcut into 40 (2" x 12½") I strips.

5. Cut two 2½" by fabric width black solid strips; subcut into 30 (2½") K squares.

6. Cut eight 2¼" by fabric width black solid strips for binding.

Completing the Strip Segments

1. Join three 1½" x 42" strips along length; press. Repeat to make five strip sets. Subcut each strip set into two 3½" x 9½" A segments (10 total) and three 3½"-square B segments (15 total) referring to Figure 1.

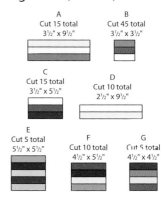

A
Cut 15 total
3½" x 9½"

B
Cut 45 total
3½" x 3½"

C
Cut 15 total
3½" x 5½"

D
Cut 10 total
2½" x 9½"

E
Cut 5 total
5½" x 5½"

F
Cut 10 total
4½" x 5½"

G
Cut 5 total
4½" x 4½"

Figure 1

2. Repeat step 1 to make three strip sets with three strips each. Subcut each strip set into five 3½" x 5½" C segments (15 total) referring to Figure 1.

3. Repeat step 1 to make three strip sets with two strips each; press. Subcut into 10 (2½" x 9½") D segments referring to Figure 1.

4. Repeat step 1 to make five strip sets with three strips each. Subcut each strip set into one 3½" x 9½" A segment (five total) and six 3½" B square segments (30 total) referring to Figure 1. ***Note:*** *You may use leftover segments to cut any of these pieces whenever possible.*

5. Repeat step 1 to make one strip set with five strips. Subcut strip set into five 5½" E square segments referring to Figure 1.

6. Repeat step 1 to make four strip sets with four strips each. Subcut strip sets into 10 (4½" x 5½") F segments and five 4½" G square segments.

Completing the Blocks

1. To complete Block 1, select and join two A segments and three B segments referring to Figure 2. Sew an H strip to opposite sides and I strips to the top and bottom of the block; press. Repeat to make five blocks.

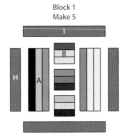

Figure 2

2. To complete Block 2, select and join three C segments with two D segments as shown in Figure 3. Add H and I strips as in step 1. Repeat to make five blocks.

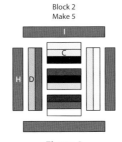

Figure 3

3. To complete Block 3, select and join one A segment with six B segments as shown in Figure 4. Add H and I strips as in step 1. Repeat to make five blocks.

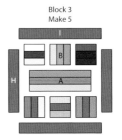

Figure 4

4. To complete Block 4, select and join one each E and G segment and two F segments as shown in Figure 5. Add H and I strips as in step 1. Repeat to make five blocks.

Figure 5

Completing the Sashing Units

1. Draw a diagonal line on the wrong side of half of the 2⅞" squares. Referring to Figure 6, place a marked square right sides together with an unmarked square and stitch ¼" on each side of the line. Cut apart on the marked line to make two J units; press open. Repeat with all squares to make 294 J units.

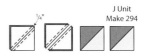

Figure 6

2. Randomly select and join six J units to make a J sashing strip as shown in Figure 7; repeat to make 49 J sashing strips.

Figure 7

Completing the Quilt

1. Arrange the blocks in five rows of four blocks each by block number referring to Figure 8 for block positioning.

Block 1	Block 2	Block 3	Block 4
Block 2	Block 3	Block 4	Block 1
Block 3	Block 4	Block 1	Block 2
Block 4	Block 1	Block 2	Block 3
Block 1	Block 2	Block 3	Block 4

Figure 8

2. Referring to the Assembly Diagram, join four blocks as arranged with five J sashing strips to make each block row. Press seams in one direction.

3. Again referring to the Assembly Diagram, join four J sashing strips with five K squares to make the sashing rows. Press seams in the opposite direction to the block rows.

4. Join the block rows and sashing rows to complete the quilt center, again referring to the Assembly Diagram.

5. Add the L, M, N and O border strips to the pieced center in alphabetical order referring to the Assembly Diagram to complete the quilt top.

6. Layer, quilt and bind referring to Finishing Your Quilt on page 160. ■

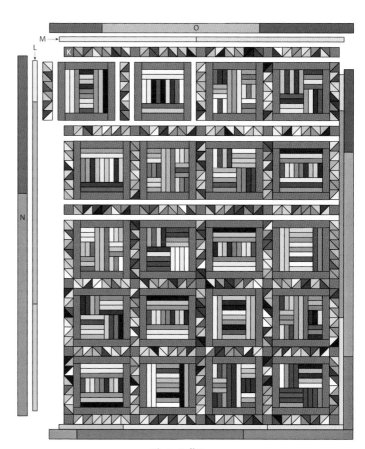

Piece-Full Days
Assembly Diagram 64" x 78"

The Colors of Butterfly Wings

Scrappy Log Cabin blocks and butterfly appliqués are the perfect blend for this bright and cheerful quilt. Choose your colors and get started.

DESIGN BY JOYCE STEWART
QUILTED BY ANN SEELY

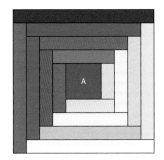

Log Cabin
8" x 8" Block
Make 52

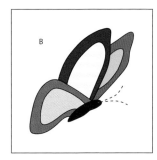

Reversed Butterfly
8" x 8" Block
Make 6

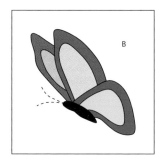

Butterfly
8" x 8" Block
Make 6

PROJECT SPECIFICATIONS

Skill Level: Intermediate
Quilt Size: 71" x 71"
Block Size: 8" x 8"
Number of Blocks: 64

MATERIALS

1 fat eighth black solid
⅔ yard aqua tonal
⅞ yard cream tonal
1⅛ yards blue print
4 yards total assorted light–medium scraps
4¼ yard total assorted medium–dark scraps
Backing 79" x 79"
Batting 79" x 79"
Thread
Thread to match appliqué fabrics
Black embroidery floss
Applique pressing sheet
3½ yards 18"-wide paper-backed fusible web
Water-erasable marker or pencil
Tracing paper
Basic sewing tools and supplies

Cutting

1. Cut eight 2¼" by fabric width aqua tonal strips for binding.

2. Cut three 8½" by fabric width cream tonal strips; subcut 12 (8½") B squares.

3. Cut eight 4" by fabric width blue print C strips.

4. Cut 52 (2½") A squares from assorted medium–dark scraps.

5. Cut appliqué pieces referring to steps 1–3 of Completing the Butterfly Blocks on page 62 using black solid and assorted light–medium and medium–dark scraps. Use remaining assorted scraps to cut 1¼"-wide strips for Log Cabin blocks.

Completing the Log Cabin Blocks

1. To complete one Log Cabin block, select one A square and one 1¼"-wide light–medium strip; sew A to the light–medium strip with right sides together as shown in Figure 1.

Figure 1

2. Trim the light–medium strip even with A at each end as shown in Figure 2; open and press seam toward the light–medium strip.

Figure 2

3. Select a second light–medium strip and place the stitched A unit right sides together on the strip with the previously stitched strip facing you as shown in Figure 3; stitch.

Figure 3

4. Trim the stitched unit as in step 2; open and press seam toward the strip.

5. Select a medium–dark strip and place the stitched A unit right sides together on the strip with the previously stitched strip facing you; stitch. Trim the stitched unit as in step 2; open and press seam toward the strip.

6. Repeat 5 with a second medium–dark strip on the remaining side of the A unit to complete one round.

7. Continue this method to add strips around A in numerical order to complete one Log Cabin block, keeping all light–medium strips on one side and all medium–dark strips on the opposite side, as shown in Figure 4.

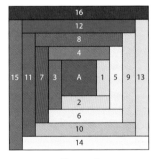

Figure 4

8. Repeat steps 1–7 to complete a total of 52 Log Cabin blocks.

9. Square up blocks to 8½" x 8½", if necessary, to finish.

Completing the Butterfly Blocks

1. Using the full-size appliqué pattern given and leaving ½" between pieces, trace six of each butterfly shape onto the paper side of the fusible web. Prepare reverse templates for each piece. Repeat to trace six of each reverse shape.

2. Cut out shapes, leaving a margin around each one; cut the inside of each shape away ¼" from the traced line to make outline shapes for each piece referring to Figure 5. **Note:** *This allows the shapes to be fused in place, but eliminates the stiffness sometimes associated with using fusible web.*

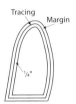

Figure 5

3. Fuse shapes to the wrong side of fabric scraps as directed on Butterfly motif; cut out shapes on traced lines. Set aside.

4. Fold each B square in half on the diagonals and crease to mark the centers.

5. Make a full-size copy of the Butterfly motif; turn the paper over and trace the design again on the paper to make a reverse copy.

6. Place the full-size Butterfly motif under the appliqué pressing sheet. Select pieces 1 and 2 and remove paper backing. Arrange and fuse these two pieces over the traced motif on top of the appliqué pressing sheet referring to Figure 6.

Figure 6

7. Continue to add and fuse pieces in numerical order to build the motif.

8. When the motif is complete, pick it up as a unit and center and fuse onto a creased B square referring to the block drawing.

9. Repeat steps 6–8 to complete six Butterfly and six Reversed Butterfly blocks.

10. Using a narrow machine blanket stitch and thread to match fabrics, stitch around edges of each fused shape.

11. Transfer antennae lines to each block using a water-erasable marker or pencil.

12. Using 3 strands black embroidery floss, stem-stitch antennae in place referring to stem-stitch diagram.

Completing the Quilt

Note: Pay very close attention to the orientation of the Log Cabin and Butterfly blocks when piecing rows.

1. Select and join eight Log Cabin blocks to make a W row as shown in Figure 7 on page 64; press seams in one direction. Repeat to make a second W row.

Designer's Tip

At some point you may prefer to stitch the strip on top of the stitched unit because it may be easier for you to control the strip on top rather than on the bottom. You may also want to stitch the same-number strip on all blocks at the same time, trim all blocks at once and then press. This is an efficient way to organize tasks, which saves time and wasted movements to and from your machine and to the cutting surface and the iron.

Figure A

2. Select and join one each Butterfly and Reversed Butterfly blocks with six Log Cabin blocks to make an X row, again referring to Figure 7; press seams in the opposite direction from the W rows. Repeat to make a reversed X row.

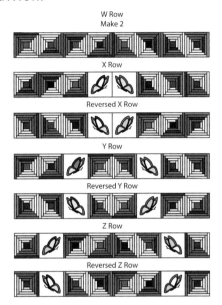

Figure 7

3. Repeat step 2 to make one each Y and Z rows and one each reversed Y and Z rows, again referring to Figure 7; press the Y row seams in the same direction as the W rows, and the Z row seams in the same direction as the X rows.

4. Arrange and join the rows referring to the Placement Diagram to complete the pieced center; press seams in one direction.

5. Join the C strips on the short ends to make one long strip; subcut strip into four 77" strips.

6. Center and sew a C strip to each side of the pieced top, stopping stitching ¼" from each corner as shown in Figure 8.

Figure 8

7. Miter corner seams as shown in Figure 9; trim mitered seam to ¼" and press open, again referring to Figure 9. Press border seams toward C strips to complete the pieced top.

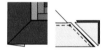

Figure 9

8. Layer, quilt and bind referring to Finishing Your Quilt on page 160. ■

The Colors of Butterfly Wings
Placement Diagram 71" x 71"

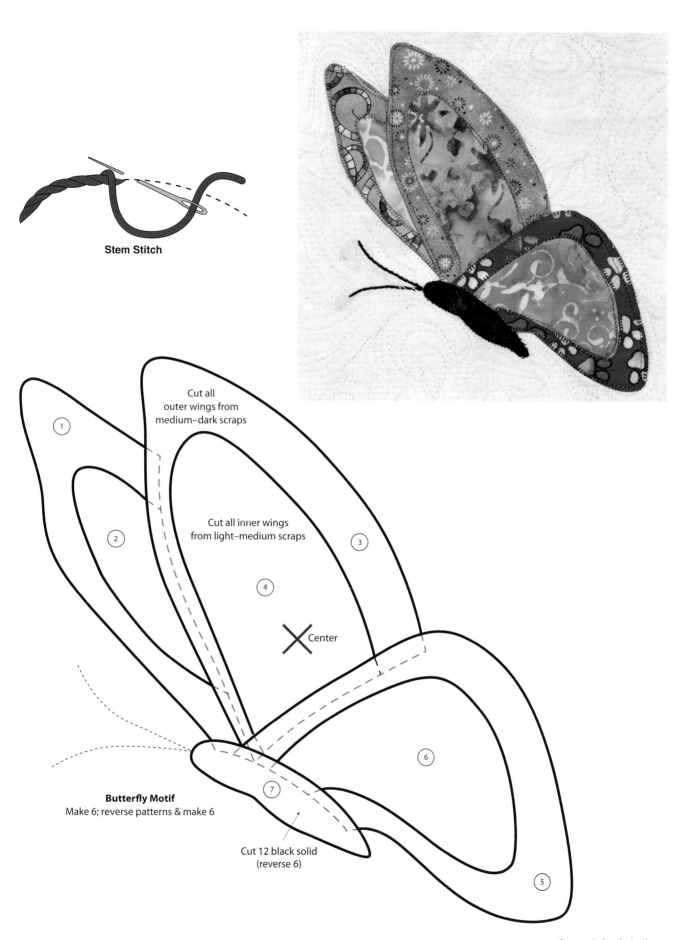

Stem Stitch

Cut all
outer wings from
medium–dark scraps

Cut all inner wings
from light–medium scraps

Center

Butterfly Motif
Make 6; reverse patterns & make 6

Cut 12 black solid
(reverse 6)

Old-Fashioned Rose Patch

Make a pretty cottage wall quilt using pastel dots and prints.

DESIGN BY ROCHELLE MARTIN

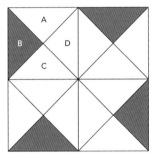

Yellow Rose Flower
8" x 8" Block
Make 4

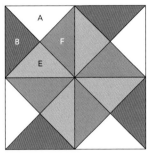

Violet Rose Flower
8" x 8" Block
Make 4

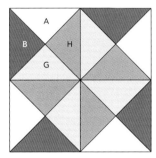

Pink Rose Flower
8" x 8" Block
Make 4

PROJECT SPECIFICATIONS

Skill Level: Beginner
Quilt Size: 42" x 42"
Block Size: 8" x 8"
Number of Blocks: 12

MATERIALS

¼ yard each violet, pink and yellow print
¼ yard each violet, pink and yellow dots
½ yard white-with-pink rose print
½ yard pink/yellow/green print
⅝ yard green dot
1⅛ yards cream tonal
Backing 48" x 48"
Batting 48" x 48"
Thread
Cream hand-quilting thread
Basic sewing tools and supplies

Cutting

1. Cut two 5¼" by fabric width strips each cream tonal (A) and green dot (B); subcut strips into (12)

5¼" squares each fabric. Cut each square on both diagonals to make 48 each A and B triangles.

2. Cut four 1½" by fabric width M strips green dot.

3. Cut one 12⅝" by fabric width strip cream tonal; subcut strip into two 12⅝" squares. Cut each square on both diagonals to make eight J triangles.

4. Cut one 8½" I square and two 6⅝" squares cream tonal. Cut the 6⅝" squares in half on one diagonal to make four K triangles.

5. Cut one 5¼" by fabric width strip each yellow (C), violet (E) and pink (G) prints; subcut strips into four 5¼" squares each fabric. Cut each square on both diagonals to make 16 each C, E and G triangles.

6. Cut one 5¼" by fabric width strip each yellow (D), violet, (F) and pink (H) dots; subcut strips into four 5¼" squares each fabric. Cut each square on both diagonals to make 16 each D, F and H triangles.

7. Cut four 3½" by fabric width L strips white-with-pink rose print.

8. Cut five 2¼" by fabric width strips pink/yellow/green print for binding.

Completing the Rose Flower Blocks

1. Sew A to B as shown in Figure 1; press seam toward B. Repeat to make 48 A-B units.

Make 48   Make 16 each

Figure 1

2. Sew C to D, E to F and G to H, again referring to Figure 1; press seams toward D, F and H. Repeat to make 16 each C-D, E-F and G-H units.

3. To complete one Yellow Rose Flower block, sew an A-B unit to a C-D unit to complete one block quarter as shown in Figure 2; press seam in one direction. Repeat to make four block quarters.

Figure 2

4. Join two block quarters to make a row as shown in Figure 3; press seam in one direction. Repeat to make two rows.

Figure 3

5. Join the rows to complete one Yellow Rose Flower block referring to the block drawing; repeat to make four blocks.

6. Repeat steps 3–5 to make four each Violet and Pink Rose Flower blocks, using E-F and G-H units with A-B units and referring to the block drawings.

Completing the Quilt

1. Arrange and join the pieced blocks with the I square and the J and K triangles in diagonal rows as shown in Figure 4; press seams in adjoining rows in opposite directions.

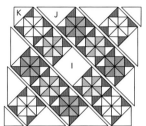

Figure 4

2. Join the pieced diagonal rows to complete the pieced center; press seams in one direction.

3. Sew an L strip to an M strip with right sides together along the length; press seams toward the M strip. Repeat to make four L-M strips.

4. Center and sew an L-M strip to each side of the pieced center, mitering corners referring to Figure 5.

Figure 5

5. Trim mitered seam to ¼" and press open to complete the pieced top, again referring to Figure 5.

6. Layer, quilt and bind referring to Finishing Your Quilt on page 160. ■

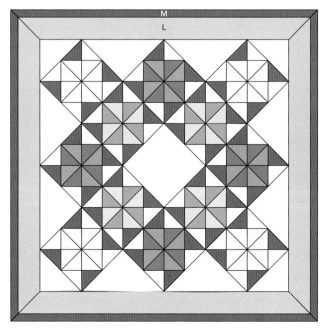

Old-Fashioned Rose Patch
Placement Diagram 42" x 42"

Happy Scrappy Houses

Happy thoughts combined with your favorite scraps will keep you inspired while working on this cute wall hanging.

DESIGN BY CONNIE KAUFFMAN

PROJECT SPECIFICATIONS

Skill Level: Intermediate
Quilt Size: 38½" x 38¼"
Block Size: 9½" x 7¾"
Number of Blocks: 9

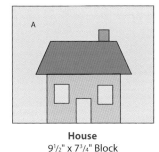

House
9½" x 7¾" Block
Make 9

MATERIALS

Assorted bright scraps for house motif appliqué
9 different scraps or 10" squares prints, solids
   or tonals
18 scraps or 10" squares bright prints
1 fat eighth yellow print
⅜ yard green tonal
⅝ yard green floral
Backing 47" x 47"
Batting 47" x 47"
Thread
1½ yards 18"-wide fusible web
Optional embellishments as instructed or desired
Basic sewing tools and supplies

Cutting

1. Prepare templates for the roof, house, door, window and chimney pieces using patterns given; trace nine each roof, house, door and chimney shapes and 18 window shapes onto the paper side of the fusible web, leaving ½" between the shapes. Cut out shapes, leaving ¼" all around.

2. Fuse shapes to the wrong side of assorted bright scraps chosen for each shape. Cut out shapes on marked lines; remove paper backing.

3. Cut one 10" x 8¼" A rectangle from each of the nine different print, solid or tonal scraps.

4. Cut 12 (2½" x 10") G strips and six 2½" x 8¼" H rectangles from 18 bright prints.

5. Cut one 2½" x 21" yellow print strip; subcut eight 2½" I squares.

6. Cut four 2¼" by fabric width green tonal strips for binding.

7. Cut two 3½" by fabric width green floral strips; subcut two 3½" x 31¾" J borders.

8. Cut two 4" by fabric width green floral strips; subcut two 4" x 39" K borders.

Completing the House Blocks

1. Fold each A rectangle on the 10" sides and crease to mark the center. Fold each house shape in half and crease.

2. To complete one House block, center and fuse a B house rectangle on A as shown in Figure 1.

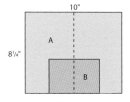

Figure 1

3. Center an E roof shape overlapping the fused house rectangle ⅛" referring to Figure 2 on page 70. Tuck the chimney behind the roof, again referring to Figure 2. Fuse roof and chimney pieces in place.

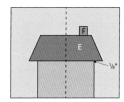

Figure 2

4. Fuse a C window shape ½" from each side and 1¾" from the bottom edge of the fused house shape as shown in Figure 3.

Figure 3

5. Center and fuse a D door shape on the fused house shape to complete the House block, again referring to Figure 3.

6. Machine buttonhole stitch around each appliqué shape using thread to match fabrics.

7. Repeat steps 4–8 to complete a total of nine House blocks.

Completing the Quilt

1. Select and join three House blocks and add an H strip to each end to make a block row as shown in Figure 4; press seams toward H and in one direction. Repeat to make three block rows.

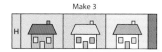

Make 3

Figure 4

2. Select and join three G strips and add an I square to each end to make a G-I sashing strip as shown in Figure 5; press seams toward G. Repeat to make four G-I sashing strips.

Make 4

Figure 5

3. Join the block rows with the G-I sashing strips to complete the pieced center referring to the Placement Diagram; press seams toward the G-I sashing strips.

4. Sew J strips to the sides and K strips to the top and bottom of the pieced center to complete the quilt top.

5. Layer, quilt and bind referring to Finishing Your Quilt on page 160.

6. Embellish each house in a different way referring to the sample quilt photo for ideas. Add lace window treatments, buttons for flowers, birds, pets, snowflakes, etc., to make a really fun and unique quilt. ◼

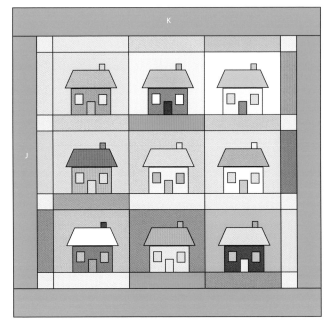

Happy Scrappy Houses
Placement Diagram 38½" x 38¼"

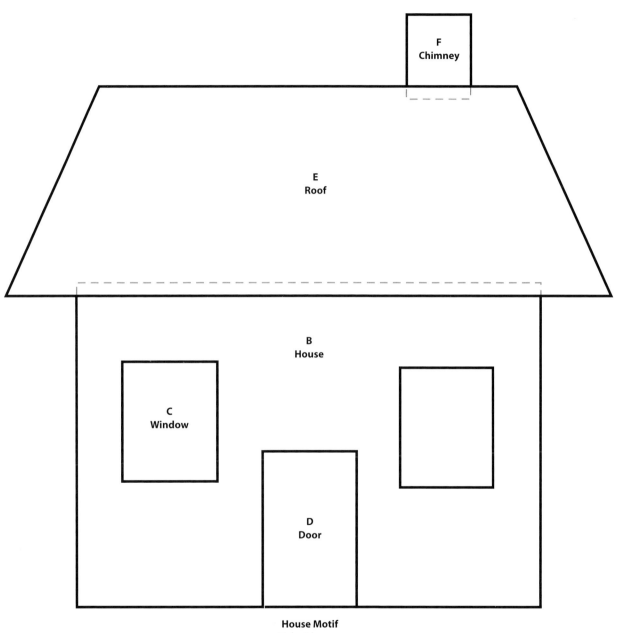

House Motif
Make 9 houses

Memories

Take all those ties and foundation-piece them into a conversation piece. This quilt would be the perfect gift for a retirement party or to remember a loved one.

DESIGN BY BEV GETSCHEL

PROJECT SPECIFICATIONS

Skill Level: Beginner
Quilt Size: 54" x 63½"
Block Size: 9½" x 9½"
Number of Blocks: 20

Memories
9½" x 9½" Block
Make 20

PROJECT NOTES

Pre-wash all flannel and silk scraps before using.

The sample quilt has no batting. The foundation flannel squares and the flannel backing make this quilt a lightweight, but warm, throw.

Using flannel for the foundation squares reduces the movement of the silk pieces during sewing.

MATERIALS

Assorted silk fabric pieces or old ties to total 5 yards
1 yard black print
3½ yards flannel
Flannel backing 62" x 72"
Thread
Basic sewing tools and supplies

Cutting

1. If using silk ties, refer to Preparing Ties for Use in Patchwork on page 77 for preparation steps. Cut prepared ties or silk fabric pieces into uneven width A strips.

2. Cut five 2½" by fabric width black print B/C strips.

3. Cut six 2¼" by fabric width black print strips for binding.

4. Cut four 7" x 60" strips along length of flannel.

5. Cut one 11" x 60" strip along length of flannel; subcut five 11" foundation squares.

6. Cut five 11" by fabric width flannel strips; subcut 15 (11") foundation squares.

Completing the Blocks

1. Select one 11" flannel foundation square.

2. Select and pin a long A strip along the diagonal of the foundation square as shown in Figure 1; trim A to a manageable length with extra extending at each end, again referring to Figure 1.

Figure 1

5. Press the top A strip to the right side as shown in Figure 4.

Figure 4

6. Continue adding strips to the foundation square in this manner until the square is completely covered as shown in Figure 5.

Figure 5

7. Trim the stitched square to 10" x 10" to complete one Memories block as shown in Figure 6.

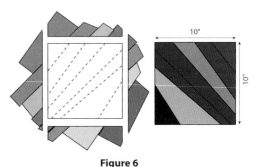

Figure 6

8. Repeat steps 1–7 to complete a total of 20 Memories blocks.

Completing the Quilt

1. Select and join four Memories blocks to make a row as shown in Figure 7; press seams open. Repeat to make a total of five rows.

Figure 7

3. Select another A strip and pin right sides together on A, trimming excess as in step 2 and referring to Figure 2.

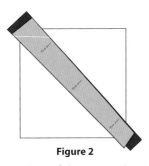

Figure 2

4. Stitch ¼" from edge of the pinned strips as shown in Figure 3.

Figure 3

Preparing Ties for Use in Patchwork

Using silk ties in quilts requires a bit of preparation.

It is best to begin with clean ties, so throw them all in the washing machine and wash on a gentle cycle and dry. The interfacing will probably bunch up, but don't worry!

After drying, open the seam that runs up the center of the back side of each tie. Remove the lining and interfacing from each one and press flat.

After pressing, you can easily determine how much of the fabric will be useful in your patchwork. At this time, you can trim the ties into uniform widths or leave as is to be used as desired in patchwork.

Now that the ties have been washed, whatever project they are used in should not shrink when washed.

Memories
Placement Diagram 54" x 63¹/₂"

2. Arrange and join the rows, turning every other row, referring to the Placement Diagram for positioning; press seams open.

3. Join the B/C strips on short ends to make one long strip; press seams open. Subcut strip into two 48" B strips and two 42½" C strips.

4. Sew B strips to opposite long sides and C strips to the top and bottom of the pieced center; press seams toward B and C strips.

5. Create four 7" x 60" crazy-patchwork strips, using the 7"-wide flannel strips and referring to steps 2–7 of Completing the Blocks; trim strips to two 6½" x 58" D strips and two 6½" x 48½" E strips.

6. Sew a D strip to the left B side of the pieced center, aligning one end of the D strip with the bottom edge of the quilt and stopping stitching 2" before the top edge of the pieced center as shown in Figure 8; press seam toward B strip.

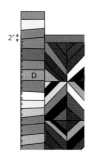

Figure 8

7. Sew an E strip to C/D before bottom edge of the pieced center; press seam toward the C/D edge.

8. Add the remaining D strip to the right edge and E strip to the top of the pieced center; press seams toward B and C strips.

9. Complete the seam on the first D strip to complete the pieced top as shown in Figure 9; press.

Figure 9

10. Layer, quilt and bind referring to Finishing Your Quilt on page 160. ■

Black & White Sawtooth

The Sawtooth block design makes a bold statement in this modern version made with black-and-white prints.

DESIGN BY SANDRA L. HATCH

PROJECT SPECIFICATIONS

Skill Level: Confident Beginner
Quilt Size: 48" x 48"
Block Size: 12" x 12"
Number of Blocks: 4

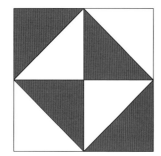

Broken Dishes
12" x 12" Block
Make 4

MATERIALS

¼ yard black solid
¾ yard total 3 different black-with-white prints
¾ yard black-and-white stripe
1¾ yards white-with-black print
Backing 54" x 54"
Batting 54" x 54"
Thread
Basic sewing tools and supplies

Cutting

1. Cut one 4½" by fabric width black solid strip; subcut four 4½" G squares.

2. Cut 19 (2½" by fabric width) black-with-white prints strips. Subcut strips into 304 (2½") C squares. Draw a diagonal line from corner to corner on the wrong side of each C square.

3. Cut nine 4½" D squares from black-with-white prints. **Note:** *The quilt would be less busy if these squares were cut from black solid.*

4. Cut eight 6⅞" squares each white-with-black and black-with-white prints. Cut each square in half on one diagonal for 16 A triangles of each color.

5. Cut 10 (4½") by fabric width white-with-black print strips; subcut strips into 152 (2½" x 4½") B rectangles.

6. Cut four 2½" by fabric width black-and-white stripe strips. Subcut two each 2½" x 36½" E strips and 2½" x 40½" F strips.

7. Cut five 2¼" by fabric width strips black-and-white stripe for binding.

Completing the Quilt

1. Sew a white-with-black A to a black-with-white A to make an A unit as shown in Figure 1; repeat for 16 A units.

Figure 1

2. Join two A units as shown in Figure 2; repeat for eight units.

Figure 2

3. Join two of the A-A units to complete one block as shown in Figure 3; repeat for four blocks. Set aside.

Figure 3

4. Place a C square on one corner of B and stitch on drawn line as shown in Figure 4; trim seam to ¼" and press to the right side as shown in Figure 5.

 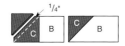

Figure 4   **Figure 5**

5. Repeat on the opposite end of B to complete a B-C unit as shown in Figure 6; repeat to make 152 B-C units.

Figure 6

6. Join three B-C units as shown in Figure 7; repeat to make 24 B-C3 units. Press seams in one direction.

Figure 7

7. Join two B-C3 units to make a B-C6 unit as shown in Figure 8; repeat for 12 B-C6 units.

Figure 8

8. Join two blocks with three B-C6 units as shown in Figure 9 to make a block row; repeat for two block rows. Press seams toward blocks.

Figure 9

9. Join two B-C6 units with three D squares to make a sashing row as shown in Figure 10; repeat for three sashing rows. Press seams toward D.

Figure 10

10. Join the block rows with the sashing rows to complete the pieced center; press seams toward block rows.

11. Sew black-and-white stripe E strips to the top and bottom and black-and-white stripe F strips to opposite sides of the pieced center; press seams toward strips.

12. Join 20 B-C units to make a side border strip as shown in Figure 11; repeat for four strips. Press seams in one direction.

Figure 11

13. Sew a B-C strip to opposite sides of the pieced top, referring to the Placement Diagram for positioning; press seams away from pieced strips.

14. Sew a G square to each end of the remaining two strips; sew to the remaining sides of the pieced center, referring to the Placement Diagram. Press seams away from pieced strips.

15. Layer, quilt and bind referring to Finishing Your Quilt on page 160. ■

Black & White Sawtooth
Placement Diagram
48" x 48"

Bed & More Quilts

Here is inspiration for countless scrappy bed quilt options.
Pick a project that suits your needs or style, and then simply add
your scraps and stash.

Peaches & Cream

Let precut 5" squares be the focal point of this quilt. It's fast, easy and really stretches your design options.

DESIGN BY CAROLYN S. VAGTS FOR THE VILLAGE PATTERN CO.

PROJECT SPECIFICATIONS

Skill Level: Confident Beginner
Quilt Size: 66" x 90"
Block Size: 8½" x 8½"
Number of Blocks: 39

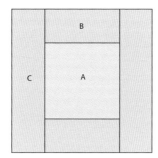

Framed Square
8½" x 8½" Block
Make 39

MATERIALS

39 precut 5" squares in wide variety of fabrics (A)
47 precut 2½" strips in shades of orange and pale greens and tans
⅝ yard coordinating narrow stripe
2⅝ yards coordinating floral
Backing 74" x 98"
Batting 74" x 98"
Neutral-color all-purpose thread
Quilting thread
Large square ruler
Basic sewing tools and supplies

Cutting

1. Cut two 2½" x 5" B rectangles and two 2½" x 9" C rectangles from 39 of the 2½"-wide strips; pin B and C together in matching sets.

2. Cut two 17¼" by fabric width strips coordinating floral; subcut strips into four 17¼" squares. Cut each square on both diagonals to make 16 D triangles.

3. Cut one 10⅞" by fabric width strip coordinating floral; subcut strip into two 10⅞" squares. Cut each square in half on one diagonal to make four E triangles.

4. Cut eight 5½" by fabric width H/I strips coordinating floral.

5. Cut seven 2½" by fabric width F/G strips coordinating narrow stripe.

Completing the Blocks

1. Select one A square and two each matching B and C rectangles (one pinned set).

2. Sew a B rectangle to opposite sides of A as shown in Figure 1; press seams toward B.

Figure 1

3. Sew C rectangles to the remaining sides of A to complete one Framed Square block referring to Figure 2; press seams toward C.

Figure 2

4. Repeat steps 1–3 to complete a total of 39 Framed Square blocks.

Completing the Quilt

1. Arrange and join the Framed Square blocks with the D triangles in diagonal rows as shown in Figure 3; press seams in adjoining rows in opposite directions. ***Note:*** *The D triangles are larger than the blocks and will overlap after joining the rows.*

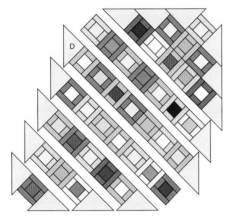

Figure 3

2. Join the rows, overlapping the triangles at the edges, again referring to Figure 3. ***Note:*** *The blocks will appear to be floating in the center with 2¼" extra at each edge.*

3. Center and sew an E triangle to each corner. Referring to Figure 4 and using a large square ruler, trim the excess of the E corner triangle even with side edges, if necessary.

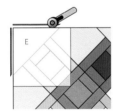

Figure 4

4. Measure the completed top through the center vertically and horizontally; it should measure 52½" x 76½". ***Note:*** *If your measurements are different, you may trim your quilt top to this size, or adjust the sizes to cut the border strips that follow.*

5. Join the F/G strips on short ends to make one long strip; press seams open. Subcut strip into two 80½" F strips and two 52½" G strips.

6. Sew the G strips to the top and bottom, and F strips to opposite long sides of the pieced center; press seams toward the F and G strips.

7. Join the H/I strips on short ends to make one long strip; press seams open. Subcut strip into two 90½" H strips and two 56½" I strips.

8. Sew the H strips to the top and bottom, and I strips to opposite sides of the pieced center to complete the pieced top; press seams toward H and I strips.

9. Use the remaining eight 2½"-wide strips for binding.

10. Layer, quilt and bind referring to Finishing Your Quilt on page 160. ■

Peaches & Cream
Placement Diagram 66" x 90"

Yukon

Make this bear-design quilt for the animal lover in your family.

DESIGN BY LUCY A. FAZELY & MICHAEL L. BURNS

PROJECT SPECIFICATIONS

Skill Level: Beginner
Quilt Size: 73" x 78"
Block Size: 10" x 15"
Number of Blocks: 15

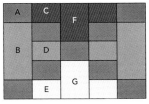

Forest Chain
10" x 15" Block
Make 8

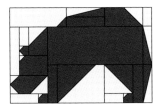

Bear
10" x 15" Block
Make 7

MATERIALS

⅜ yard dark green tonal
½ yard gray print
⅝ yard black tonal
⅝ yard medium green print
¾ yard red tonal
1¼ yards cream/brown toile
2 yards dark brown tonal
2 yards bear print
Backing 79" x 84"
Batting 79" x 84"
Neutral color all-purpose thread
Quilting thread
Basting spray
Basic sewing tools and supplies

Cutting

1. Cut nine 2½" by fabric width A strips red tonal.

2. Cut two 6½" by fabric width B strips medium green print.

3. Cut two 2½" by fabric width D strips medium green print.

4. Cut two 2½" by fabric width C strips dark green tonal.

5. Cut one 4½" by fabric width F strip dark green tonal.

6. Cut five 2½" by fabric width strips cream/brown toile; set aside two strips for E. Subcut the remaining three strips into seven 6½" I pieces and 21 (2½") L squares. Mark a diagonal line from corner to corner on the wrong side of each L square.

7. Cut three 4½" by fabric width strips cream/brown toile. Prepare template for J using pattern given; cut J and JR pieces from one strip using the template. Set aside one strip for G; subcut the remaining strip into seven 5½" V pieces.

8. Cut one 3⅞" by fabric width strip cream/brown toile; subcut strip into four 3⅞" Y squares. Cut each square in half on one diagonal to make seven Y triangles; discard remaining triangle.

9. Cut four 1½" by fabric width strips cream/brown toile; subcut strips into seven 5½" R pieces, seven 3½" T pieces, 21 (2½") N pieces, 14 (1½") S squares and seven 1¼" Q squares. Draw a diagonal line from corner to corner on the wrong side of each Q and S square.

10. Cut one 1" by fabric width strip cream/brown toile; subcut strip into 28 (1") P squares. Mark a diagonal line from corner to corner on the wrong side of each square.

11. Cut five 4½" by fabric width strips dark brown tonal; cut J and JR pieces from one strip using the template. Subcut the remaining strips into seven 4½" W squares, 21 (1½") K pieces and seven 10½" U pieces.

12. Cut three 2½" by fabric width strips dark brown tonal; subcut strips into 14 (3½") O pieces and 14 (4½") M pieces.

13. Cut one 1½" by fabric width strip dark brown tonal; subcut strip into 28 (1½") H squares. Draw a diagonal line from corner to corner on the wrong side of seven squares.

14. Cut one 3⅞" by fabric width strip dark brown tonal; subcut strip into four 3⅞" X squares. Cut each square in half on one diagonal to make seven X triangles; discard remaining triangle.

15. Cut one 10½" by fabric width strip dark brown tonal; subcut strip into four 10½" HH squares.

16. Cut eight 2¼" by fabric width strips dark brown tonal for binding.

17. Cut 10 (1½") by fabric width strips black tonal. Join strips on short ends to make one long strip; press seams open. Subcut strip into two each 50½" Z strips, 47½" AA strips, 56½" DD strips and 53½" EE strips.

18. Cut five 2½" by fabric width strips gray print. Join strips on short ends to make one long strip; press seams open. Subcut strip into two 52½" BB strips and two 51½" CC strips.

19. Cut six 10½" by fabric width strips bear print. Join strips on short ends to make one long strip; press seams open. Subcut strip into two 58½" FF strips and two 53½" GG strips.

Completing the Forest Chain Blocks

1. Sew a B strip between two A strips with right sides together along the length to make a strip set; press seams toward B. Repeat to make two A-B strip sets.

2. Subcut the A-B strip sets into 16 (3½") A-B units as shown in Figure 1.

Figure 1

3. Sew a C strip to an A strip to a D strip to an A strip to an E strip with right sides together along the length to make a strip set; press seams in one direction. Repeat to make two A-C-D-E strip sets.

4. Subcut the A-C-D-E strip sets into 16 (3½") A-C-D-E units as shown in Figure 2.

Figure 2

5. Sew an A strip between an F and G strip with right sides together along the length; press seams toward A.

6. Subcut the A-F-G strip set into eight 3½" A-F-G units.

7. Join two A-B units with two A-C-D-E units and one A-F-G unit to complete one Forest Chain block as shown in Figure 3; press seams away from the center unit. Repeat to make eight blocks.

Figure 3

Completing the Bear Blocks

1. Referring to Figure 4, place a marked H square right sides together on one corner of I; stitch on the marked line. Trim seam allowance to ¼"; press H to the right side to complete an H-I unit. Repeat for seven H-I units.

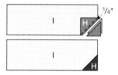

Figure 4

2. Sew a dark brown tonal J to a cream/brown toile J to make a J unit as shown in Figure 5; repeat to make 14 J units. Press seams toward dark brown tonal J pieces. Repeat with JR pieces to make seven JR units.

Figure 5

3. Sew K to the dark side of the J and JR units as shown in Figure 6; press seams toward K.

Figure 6

4. Sew L to M to make an L-M unit as in step 1 and referring to Figure 7; repeat to make 14 L-M units.

Figure 7

5. Sew an H-I unit to a J-K unit to an L-M unit and add N to make the top row as shown in Figure 8; repeat to make seven top rows. Set aside.

Figure 8

6. Sew S to the remaining L-M units as in step 1 and referring to Figure 9 to make seven L-M-S units.

Figure 9

7. Sew P to H as in step 1 and referring to Figure 10 to make 21 H-P units; add a second P to seven H-P units to make H-P-P units, again referring to Figure 10.

Figure 10

8. Sew Q to O as in step 1 and referring to Figure 11 to make seven O-Q units.

Figure 11

9. Sew L to O referring to step 1 and Figure 12 to make seven L-O units.

Figure 12

10. Referring to Figure 13, sew T to one H-P unit; press seam toward T. Repeat to make seven units.

Figure 13

11. Sew the L-M-S unit to the T-H-P unit to make a snout unit referring to Figure 14; press seam toward the L-M-S unit. Repeat to make seven snout units.

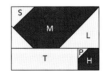
Figure 14

12. Referring to Figure 15, sew N to an H-P-P unit; add an L-M unit. Sew an O-Q unit to the M edge of the second unit and add R to complete the ear unit, again

referring to Figure 15; press seams toward O-Q and R. Repeat to make seven ear units.

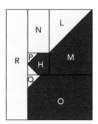
Figure 15

13. Sew an ear unit to a snout unit to complete a head unit; press seams toward the ear unit. Repeat to make seven head units.

14. Referring to step 1 and Figure 16, sew W to V; add K to make a front-leg unit. Press seams toward K; repeat to make seven front-leg units.

Figure 16

15. Sew X to Y; press seam toward X. Repeat to make seven X-Y units.

16. Sew N to an H-P unit; press seam toward N. Sew the N-H-P unit to the X-Y unit; add a JR-K unit to complete a hind-leg unit as shown in Figure 17; press seam toward the JR-K unit.

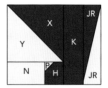
Figure 17

17. Join the front-leg and hind-leg units to complete a leg unit; press seam toward the front-leg unit. Repeat to make seven leg units.

18. Sew a J unit to one end of U as shown in Figure 18 to make the body unit; press seam toward U. Repeat to make seven body units.

Figure 18

19. Arrange and join the pieced units as shown in Figure 19 to complete one Bear block; press seams toward the largest unpieced units. Repeat to make seven Bear blocks.

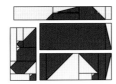

Figure 19

Completing the Quilt

1. Join one Bear block and two Forest Chain blocks to make an XX row as shown in Figure 20; press seams toward the Forest Chain blocks. Repeat to make three XX rows.

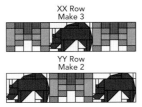

XX Row
Make 3

YY Row
Make 2

Figure 20

2. Join one Forest Chain block with two Bear blocks to make a YY row, again referring to Figure 20; press seams toward the Forest Chain blocks. Repeat to make two YY rows.

3. Join the XX and YY rows referring to the Placement Diagram for positioning of rows; press seams in one direction.

4. Sew Z–FF border strips to the pieced center referring to the Placement Diagram for positioning; press seams away from the pieced center.

5. Sew an HH square to each end of each GG strip; press seams toward the GG strips.

6. Sew the HH-GG strips to the top and bottom of the pieced center to complete the pieced top; press seams toward the HH-GG strips.

7. Layer, quilt and bind referring to Finishing Your Quilt on page 160. ■

Yukon
Placement Diagram 73" x 78"

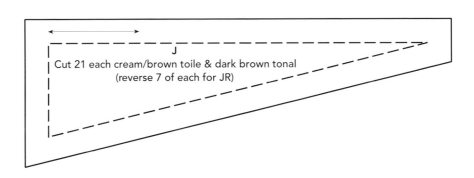

J
Cut 21 each cream/brown toile & dark brown tonal
(reverse 7 of each for JR)

Cross Ties

Don't have access to the Creative Grid Ruler? Not a problem. Follow these alternate instructions using the template provided.

DESIGN BY KATHY BROWN

PROJECT SPECIFICATIONS

Skill Level: Confident Beginner
Quilt Size: 52" x 60"
Block Size: 8" x 8"
Number of Blocks: 30

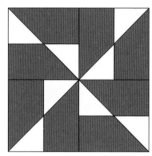

Dark Cross Ties
8" x 8" Block
Make 15

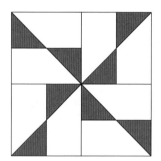

Light Cross Ties
8" x 8" Block
Make 15

MATERIALS

⅛ yard each 15 coordinating dark fabrics
⅛ yard each 15 coordinating light fabrics
½ yard dark brown print
1⅓ yards burgundy print
Backing 60" x 68"
Batting 60" x 68"
Thread
Basic sewing tools and supplies

Cutting

1. Cut one 2½" by fabric width A strip from each of the coordinating dark fabrics.

2. Cut one 2½" by fabric width B strip from each of the coordinating light fabrics.

3. Cut five 2½" by fabric width dark brown print C/D strips.

4. Cut six 4½" by fabric width burgundy print E strips.

5. Cut six 2½" by fabric width burgundy print strips for binding.

Creating the A & B Triangle Sets

1. Select one each A and B strip. Sew together along length to make an A-B strip set. Repeat with all A-B strips to make 15 strip sets. Press seams toward darker strips.

2. Prepare a template using the pattern given; transfer seam, matching lines to the template.

3. Place the template on the strip right side up and trace or cut to result in an A triangle set as shown in Figure 1. Flip the template over and align the bottom edge with the opposite side of the strip and trace to cut a B triangle set. Continue across the strip to yield eight each A and B triangle sets as shown in Figure 2.

Figure 1

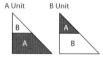

Figure 2

4. Separate the A and B triangle sets into separate piles.

5. Repeat steps 3 and 4 with the remaining 14 strip sets to result in 15 piles each A and B triangle sets.

Designer's Tip

To avoid distortion, heavily starch the 2½"-wide strips before stitching together. This will stabilize the bias edges that will be stitched together to make the blocks.

Completing the Blocks

1. Select two matching A triangle sets from one pile; stitch these two sets together to make an A unit as shown in Figure 3; press seam in one direction referring to Figure 4. ***Note:*** *The seams on the right side will not match; do not pin the seams to match. Be sure to align the square corners and the side and bottom edges of triangles when stitching.* Repeat to make a total of four matching A units from this same pile.

Figure 3   **Figure 4**

2. Lay out the four A units as shown in Figure 5. Join to make two rows; press seams in alternate directions. Join the rows to complete one Dark Cross Ties block as shown in Figure 6; press seam in one direction.

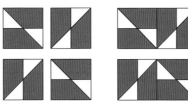

Figure 5   **Figure 6**

3. Repeat steps 1 and 2 to complete 15 Dark Cross Ties blocks.

4. Repeat steps 1 and 2 with the B triangle sets to complete 15 Light Cross Ties blocks referring to Figure 7.

Figure 7

Completing the Top

1. Using a design wall or other flat surface, lay out the blocks, alternating light and dark blocks, to make six rows of five blocks each referring to the Placement Diagram for positioning. When satisfied with positioning, join the blocks in rows; press seams in adjacent rows in opposite directions.

2. Join the rows to complete the quilt center; press seams in one direction.

3. Join the C/D strips on short ends to make one long strip; press seams open. Subcut strip into two 48½" C strips and two 44½". D strips.

4. Sew a C strip to opposite long sides and D strips to the top and bottom of the pieced center; press seams toward C and D strips.

5. Join the E strips on short ends to make one long strip; press seams open. Subcut into four 52½" E strips.

6. Sew an E strip to opposite long sides and to the top and bottom of the pieced center; press seams toward E strips.

7. Layer, quilt and bind referring to Finishing Your Quilt on page 160. ■

Cross Ties
Placement Diagram 52" x 60"

Match line to strip set seam

A/B
Cut 120 each A & B triangle sets
referring to Figures 1 & 2

When printing patterns, check to make sure
your print settings are set to print at 100
percent and page scaling displays "None."

Fractured Stars

Bright yellow and orange pieces create the blades in this unusual star design.

DESIGN BY KATE LAUCOMER

PROJECT SPECIFICATIONS

Skill Level: Intermediate
Quilt Size: 40" x 40"
Block Size: 10" x 10"
Number of Blocks: 16

MATERIALS

1¼ yards medium orange
   tonal
1¼ yards bright yellow dot
2¼ yards dark orange tonal
Backing 46" x 46"
Batting 46" x 46"
Neutral color all-purpose thread
Quilting thread
Basic sewing tools and supplies

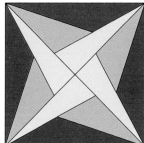

Fractured Star
10" x 10" Block

Cutting

1. Make 65 copies of the paper-piecing pattern given.

2. Cut four 2¼" by fabric width strips dark orange tonal for binding.

Completing the Blocks

1. Cut apart one copy of the paper-piecing pattern on the solid lines as shown in Figure 1.

Figure 1   **Figure 2**

2. Use each piece to rough-cut a fabric piece as shown in Figure 2, placing the pattern on the wrong side of the fabric and cutting the pieces at least ¼" larger all around than the paper piece to allow for seam allowance and to allow a bit of leeway in arranging the pieces before stitching.

3. Place fabric to cover area 1 on another paper pattern with wrong side of fabric against the unmarked side of the paper, allowing fabric to extend at least ¼" into adjacent areas as shown in Figure 3.

Figure 3

4. Place fabric for area 2 right sides together with fabric 1 on the 1-2 edge as shown in Figure 4; pin along the 1-2 line. Fold fabric 2 over to cover area 2, allowing fabric to extend at least ¼" into adjacent areas as shown in Figure 5. Adjust fabric if necessary. Unfold fabric 2; pin to lie flat on piece 1.

Figure 4   **Figure 5**

5. Flip paper pattern; stitch on the 1-2 line, beginning and ending 2 or 3 stitches into adjacent areas as shown in Figure 6. Stitch to (or beyond) the outside heavy solid line on outer areas as shown in Figure 7.

Figure 6   **Figure 7**

6. Trim the 1-2 seam allowance to ⅛"–¼" as shown in Figure 8. Fold fabric 2 to cover area 2; lightly press with a warm dry iron.

Figure 8

7. Continue to add fabrics in numerical order to cover the paper pattern as shown in Figure 9. Check that each piece will cover its area before stitching. **Note:** *The very short stitches are hard to remove and often cause a tear in the paper pattern. Should this happen, place a small piece of transparent tape over the tear to continue to use the pattern. Do not use this quick fix frequently, as it makes removal of the paper difficult.*

Figure 9

8. Trim paper and fabric edges even on the outside heavy solid line as shown in Figure 10.

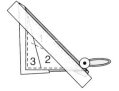

Figure 10

9. Complete 64 paper-pieced sections.

10. Place two block sections fabric sides together. Stick a pin through both sections at each end of the dashed seam line to be sure the lines on both sections match as shown in Figure 11. Stitch along the dashed seam lines to join the sections as shown in Figure 12. Remove paper from seam-allowance area only; press seam to one side.

Figure 11   **Figure 12**

11. Join two more sections; press. Join the two joined sections to complete one block referring to the block drawing; press seams to one side. Repeat for 16 blocks. **Note:** *Leave paper pattern intact until the blocks are joined.*

Completing the Quilt

1. Join four blocks to make a row as shown in Figure 13; repeat for four rows. Press seams in adjoining rows in opposite directions.

Figure 13

2. Join the rows to complete the pieced top; press seams in one direction.

3. Remove all paper pieces.

4. Layer, quilt and bind referring to Finishing Your Quilt on page 160. ■

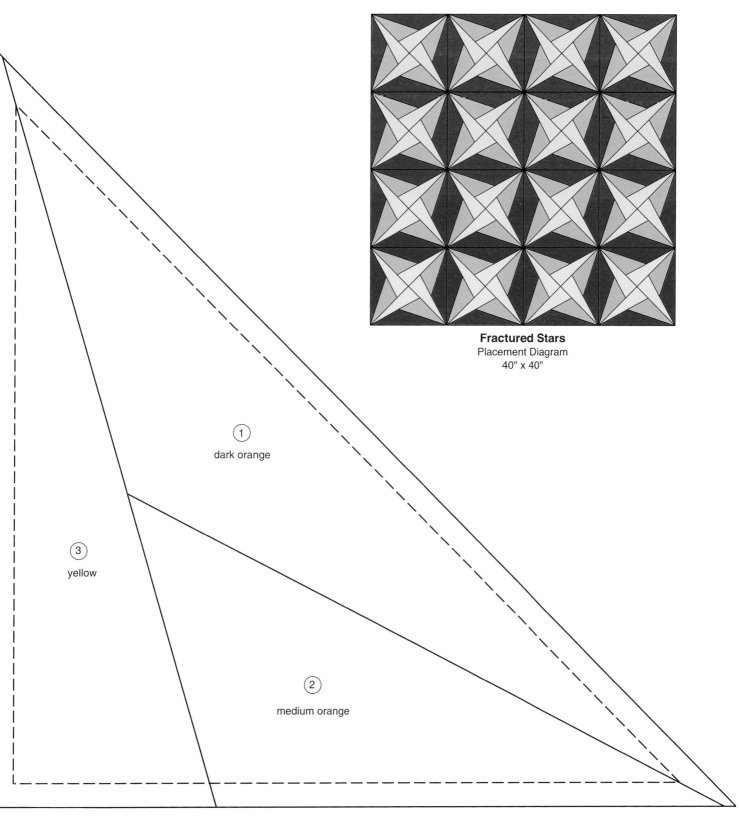

Fractured Stars
Placement Diagram
40" x 40"

①
dark orange

③
yellow

②
medium orange

Paper-Piecing Pattern
Make 64 copies

Pedaling Petals

Create a stunning quilt with quick and easy layered fusible appliqué flowers placed on a simple pieced background.

DESIGN BY CARA GULATI

PROJECT SPECIFICATIONS

Skill Level: Intermediate
Quilt Size: 87½" x 105"

MATERIALS

⅓ yard black print
⅝ yard each 5 different stripes
⅝ yard each 10 bright tonals
¾ yard yellow tonal
2¼ yards each 2 different brown tonals
2¼ yards each 2 different gray tonals
Backing 94" x 111"
Batting 94" x 111"
Neutral color all-purpose thread
Quilting thread
Invisible thread
Freezer paper
Pencil and string
Water-soluble glue stick
Basic sewing tools and supplies

Cutting

1. Cut eight 18" squares each from one gray (A) and one brown (B) tonal; cut seven squares each from the second gray (A) and second brown (B) tonal to total 30 squares.

2. Prepare templates for appliqué using patterns given.

3. Create a complete petal pattern using the template given as shown in Figure 1.

Figure 1

4. Trace the petal and C shapes onto the dull side of freezer paper referring to pattern for number to cut; copy directional arrow onto petal template. Cut out pieces.

5. Center the shiny side of the C circles on the wrong side of the black print motifs, leaving ½" between motifs for seam allowance as shown in Figure 2; press to hold in place. **Note:** *The fabric used has a 3" motif that will fit inside the 4" circle. If your fabric does not have a motif, simply place on fabric with ½" between pieces.*

Figure 2

6. Cut out C circles, adding a ¼" seam allowance all around as shown in Figure 3.

Figure 3

7. Using the pencil with an 8" length of string, draw (20) 16" D circles on the freezer paper as shown in Figure 4; cut two D circles from each of the 10 tonals referring to steps 5 and 6, adding a ¼" seam allowance all around.

Figure 4

8. Align the directional arrow on freezer-paper petal pieces on the wrong side of fabric stripes, press to hold in place and cut as directed on pattern, adding a ¼" seam allowance all around.

9. Cut (10) 2¼" by fabric width strips yellow tonal for binding.

Completing the Background

1. Arrange the A and B squares in six rows of five squares each, alternating the positioning of A and B referring to the Placement Diagram.

2. When satisfied with the arrangement, join squares in rows; press seams in one direction, alternating the direction from row to row. Join the rows to complete the pieced background; press seams in one direction.

Completing the Quilt

1. Using the glue stick, place glue around the outer edge on the freezer-paper shapes as shown in Figure 5.

Figure 5

2. Use your thumb or forefinger to push the seam allowance of the fabric over the edge of the freezer-paper template and stick it to the glue. Work your way around the circle until the edge is completely turned. Repeat with all shapes. ***Note:*** *Clip into the inside corners of the petal shapes to allow the edges to lay smooth.*

3. Set up your sewing machine with invisible thread in the top of the machine and in the bobbin. Reduce the tension to about halfway between zero and normal. Set the machine to zigzag with stitch size about 1/16" length and width. ***Note:*** *Wind the bobbin very slowly, and fill only halfway.*

4. Center C right side up on the right side of one petal shape as shown in Figure 6; pin to hold. Zigzag-stitch to hold in place.

Figure 6   Figure 7

5. Place the appliquéd unit on a second petal shape with lower petals between spaces in upper petals as shown in Figure 7. Zigzag-stitch along overlapping edges to hold to complete a flower unit, again referring to Figure 7. Repeat to make 20 flower units.

6. Arrange the flower units on the D circles; pin pleasing sets to hold.

7. Select one set; unpin. Fold flower unit and D in quarters and crease to mark the centers as shown in Figure 8.

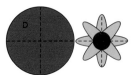

Figure 8

8. Unfold and center the flower unit on the D circle as shown in Figure 9; stitch in place as in step 4 to complete one flower circle. Repeat to make 20 flower circles.

Figure 9   Figure 10

9. Center and pin the flower circles at the intersections of the A and B squares on the pieced background as shown in Figure 10 and referring to the Placement Diagram.

10. Stitch flower circles in place as in step 4 to complete the quilt top.

11. Cut away the background fabric from behind each appliqué piece, leaving a 1/4" seam allowance around the inside edge of the stitching as shown in Figure 11.

Figure 11

12. Place the quilt top in a bathtub with paper side facing up; wet it down. Wait a few minutes, and then pull out freezer-paper pieces.

13. Continue to cut away background layers and remove paper from each layer, wetting down as needed.

14. Let the quilt top dry; press carefully.

15. Layer, quilt and bind referring to Finishing Your Quilt on page 160. ■

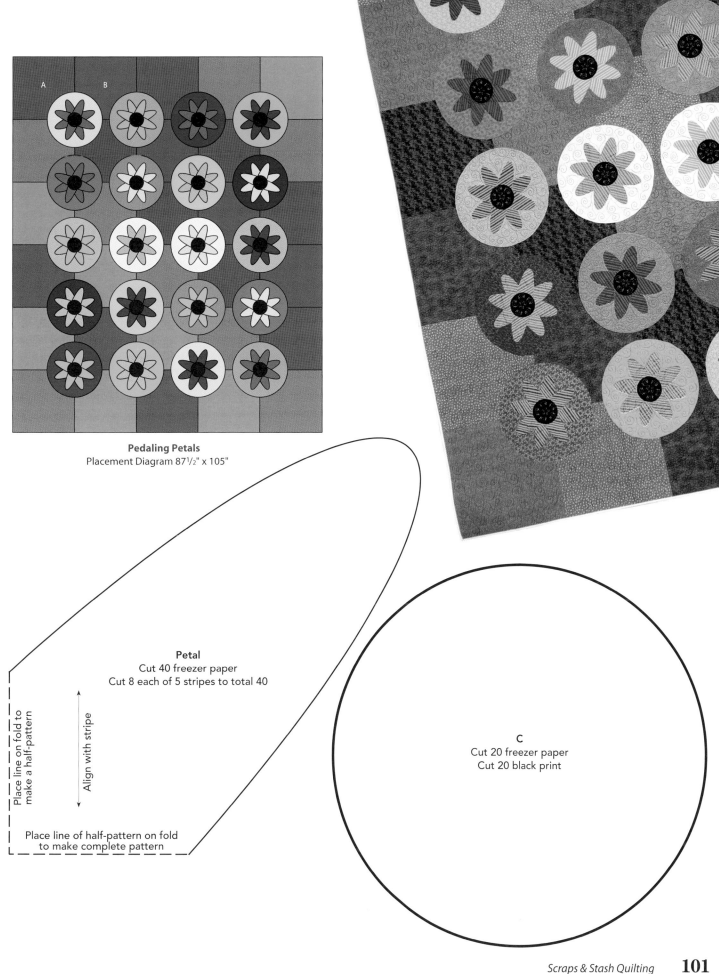

Pedaling Petals
Placement Diagram 87¹/₂" x 105"

Petal
Cut 40 freezer paper
Cut 8 each of 5 stripes to total 40

Place line on fold to make a half-pattern

Align with stripe

Place line of half-pattern on fold
to make complete pattern

C
Cut 20 freezer paper
Cut 20 black print

Yo-Yo Bedwarmer

Use a large-scale fabric and make this the focal point of any bedroom.

DESIGN BY CHRIS MALONE

PROJECT SPECIFICATIONS

Skill Level: Beginner
Project Size: 80" x 16" without leaves
Finished Yo-Yo Size: 4"-diameter

PROJECT NOTES

If the usable width of the large floral print is less than 42", you may need more yardage. The 4-yard requirement is based on cutting five 8¼"-diameter circles across the width of the fabric.

In choosing a large-scale floral for this project, remember that the actual shapes will be lost in the gathers; just the colors will be visible. Choosing a palette of several colors, that blend will be restful to the eye. Conversely, choosing a print with only two or three strongly contrasting colors will be more dynamic but could also look splotchy.

We recommend that you make one yo-yo from your chosen fabric to see if you like it before cutting out all 80 circles.

MATERIALS

½ yard green tonal
4 yards large floral print
18" x 22" fleece rectangle
Thread
Compass
Template material
Beeswax (optional)
Basic sewing tools and supplies

Preparing the Yo-Yos

1. Using the compass, draw an 8¼"-diameter circle on the template material; cut out to make the circle template.

2. Use the template to draw 80 circles on the wrong side of the large floral print; cut out circles on traced lines.

3. Cut a length of thread to match the fabric; double thread and knot the ends together.

4. Working with the wrong side of one yo-yo shape facing you, turn under ¼" to the wrong side and insert the needle near the folded edge as shown in Figure 1.

Figure 1

5. Sew a basic running stitch about ⅜" long around the edge of the circle, turning the edge under as you sew. Stop stitching when you reach the beginning knot.

Designer's Tip

Strengthen the thread used to gather the yo-yos, run each length used through a piece of beeswax.

6. Pull the thread to gather the circle as tightly as you can and move the hole to the center of the circle as shown in Figure 2.

Figure 2

7. Insert the needle between two gathers to the back of the yo-yo and make several small knots to secure; clip thread.

8. Use your fingers to press the yo-yo flat with the hole in the center as shown in Figure 3.

Figure 3

9. Repeat steps 3–8 to make a total of 80 yo-yos.

Completing the Top

1. Select four yo-yos for a vertical row. Hold two yo-yos with right sides together; whipstitch together right at the edge with about eight close stitches to cover about ¼" using a waxed doubled thread as shown in Figure 4.

Figure 4

2. Unfold the joined pair and add a third yo-yo in the same manner. Continue with the fourth yo-yo to complete one vertical row as shown in Figure 5.

Figure 5

3. Repeat steps 1 and 2 to complete a total of 20 vertical rows.

4. Join two vertical rows with right sides together in the same manner as joining the yo-yos; continue joining the rows until all rows are joined to complete the top.

Completing the Leaves

1. Prepare a template for the leaf shape using the pattern given.

2. To make leaves, draw 12 leaf shapes onto the wrong side of one end of the green tonal, leaving ⅜" between shapes.

3. Fold the fabric in half, right sides together, with the drawn shapes on top; pin the folded layers to the fleece. Sew around each leaf shape, leaving an opening where indicated on pattern and referring to Figure 6.

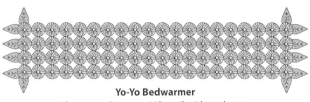

Yo-Yo Bedwarmer
Placement Diagram 80" x 16" without leaves

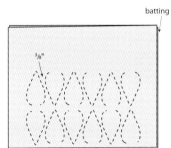

Figure 6

4. Cut out each leaf ⅛" from stitched lines; clip curves and turn right side out through the bottom opening.

5. Fold in the seam allowances on the openings and hand-stitch the openings closed; press flat.

6. Transfer the vein lines to the top of each leaf; stitch on the lines two times to quilt.

7. Using the photo and Placement Diagram as guides for positioning, arrange and hand-stitch six leaves at each end of the stitched yo-yo top, placing the rounded ends under the yo-yos about 1" as shown in Figure 7 to finish. ◼

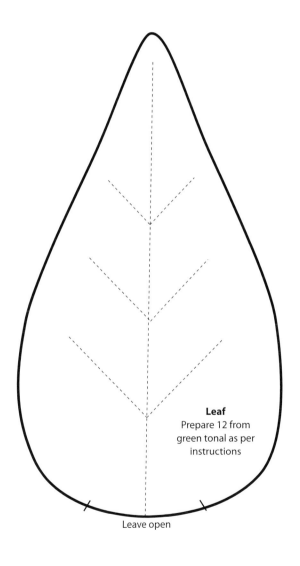

Leaf
Prepare 12 from green tonal as per instructions

Leave open

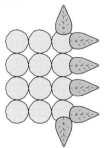

Figure 7

Almost Amish

The black used in old Amish quilts made the other colors more vibrant, just as it does in this quilt.

DESIGN BY CATE TALLMAN-EVANS

PROJECT SPECIFICATIONS

Skill Level: Intermediate
Quilt Size: 75½" x 99½"
Block Size: 12" x 12"
Number of Blocks: 35

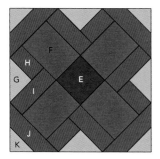

Geneva Cross
12" x 12" Block
Make 18

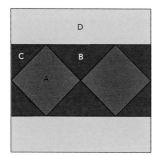

Broken Sash
12" x 12" Block
Make 17

MATERIALS

1⅛ yards light rust tonal
1¼ yards purple tonal
1⅝ yards pink tonal
1¾ yards multicolored floral
1⅞ yards gold tonal
2 yards black solid
Backing 82" x 106"
Batting 82" x 106"
Thread
Basic sewing tools and supplies

Cutting

1. Cut five 4¾" by fabric width strips pink tonal; subcut strips into 34 (4¾") A squares.

2. Cut six 4¾" by fabric width strips pink tonal; subcut strips into 72 (3½" x 4¾") F rectangles.

3. Cut two 7¼" by fabric width strips purple tonal; subcut strips into nine 7¼" squares. Cut each square on both diagonals to make 36 B triangles; set aside two triangles for another project.

4. Cut four 3⅞" by fabric width strips purple tonal; subcut strips into 34 (3⅞") squares. Cut each square in half on one diagonal to make 68 C triangles.

5. Cut two 3½" by fabric width strips purple tonal; subcut strips into 18 (3½") E squares.

6. Cut three 12½" by fabric width strips gold tonal; subcut strips into 34 (3½" x 12½") D strips.

7. Cut nine 2¼" by fabric width strips gold tonal for binding.

8. Cut three 5½" by fabric width strips light rust tonal; subcut strips into 18 (5½") squares. Cut each square on both diagonals to make 72 G triangles.

9. Cut five 2⅝" by fabric width strips light rust tonal; subcut strips into 72 (2⅝") K squares. Draw a diagonal line from corner to corner on the wrong side of each square.

10. Cut three 3½" by fabric width strips black solid; subcut strips into 72 (1¾" x 3½") H rectangles.

11. Cut three 4¾" by fabric width strips black solid; subcut strips into 72 (1¾" x 4¾") I rectangles.

12. Cut five 4¾" by fabric width strips black solid; subcut strips into 36 (4¾") squares. Cut each square in half on one diagonal to make 72 J triangles.

13. Cut eight 1¾" by fabric width strips black solid. Join strips on the short ends to make one long strip; press seams open. Subcut strip into two 84½" L strips and two 63" M strips.

14. Cut eight 7" by fabric width strips multicolored floral. Join strips on the short ends to make one long strip; press seams open. Subcut strip into two 87" N strips and two 76" O strips.

Completing the Broken Sash Blocks

1. To complete one Broken Sash block, sew C to two adjacent sides of A and add B to make an A-B-C unit as shown in Figure 1; press seams away from A. Repeat to make two A-B-C units.

Figure 1

2. Join the A-B-C units to make the center row as shown in Figure 2; press seam in one direction.

Figure 2

3. Sew D to opposite sides of the center row referring to the block drawing to complete the block; press seams toward D. Repeat to make 17 blocks.

Completing the Geneva Cross Blocks

1. To complete one Geneva Cross block, sew H to one short side of G and add I to the remaining short side of G to complete a G-H-I unit as shown in Figure 3; press seams toward H and then I. Repeat to make four units.

Figure 3

2. Sew a G-H-I unit to opposite sides of F to make a side unit as shown in Figure 4; press seams toward F. Repeat to make two side units.

Figure 4

3. Place K right sides together with J as shown in Figure 5; stitch on the marked line. Trim seam to ¼" and press K to the right side to complete a J-K unit, again referring to Figure 5. Repeat to make four J-K units.

Figure 5

4. Sew a J-K unit to each side unit to complete the corner units as shown in Figure 6; press seams toward the J-K units.

Figure 6

5. Sew F to opposite sides of E to make the center row as shown in Figure 7; press seams toward F.

Figure 7

6. Sew a corner unit to opposite sides of the center row as shown in Figure 8; press seams toward the corner units.

Figure 8

7. Sew the remaining J-K units to the stitched unit to complete the block as shown in Figure 9; press seams toward the J-K units. Repeat to make 18 blocks.

Figure 9

Completing the Quilt

1. Join three Geneva Cross blocks with two Broken Sash blocks to make an X row as shown in Figure 10; press seams toward the Broken Sash blocks. Repeat to make four X rows.

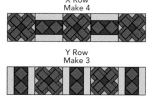

X Row
Make 4

Y Row
Make 3

Figure 10

2. Join three Broken Sash blocks with two Geneva Cross blocks to make a Y row, again referring to Figure 10; press seams toward the Broken Sash blocks. Repeat to make three Y rows.

3. Join the X and Y rows to complete the pieced center referring to the Placement Diagram for positioning of rows; press seams in one direction.

4. Sew an L strip to opposite long sides and M strips to the top and bottom of the pieced center; press seams toward the L and M strips.

5. Sew an N strip to opposite long sides and O strips to the top and bottom of the pieced center; press seams toward the N and O strips.

6. Layer, quilt and bind referring to Finishing Your Quilt on page 160. ■

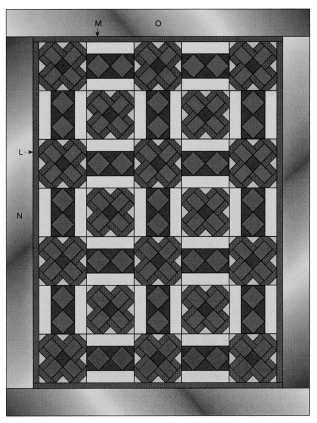

Almost Amish
Placement Diagram 75¹/₂" x 99¹/₂"

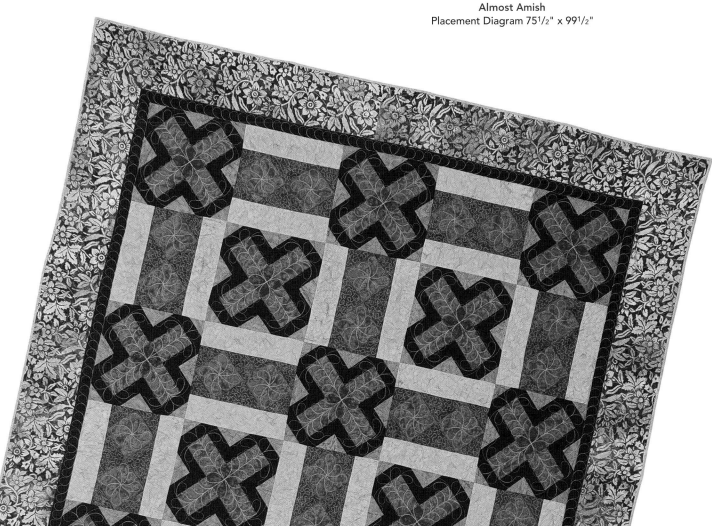

Forever Spring Bed Runner

Spread a bit of spring across the end of your bed with precut 5" squares.

DESIGN BY CAROLYN S. VAGTS FOR THE VILLAGE PATTERN CO.

PROJECT SPECIFICATIONS

Skill Level: Beginner
Bed Runner Size: 87¾" x 20¾"

MATERIALS

54 precut 5" squares (A)
¾ yard light coordinating fabric
⅞ yard dark coordinating fabric
Batting 94" x 29"
Backing 94" x 29"
Neutral-color all-purpose thread
Quilting thread
Basic sewing tools and supplies

Cutting

1. Cut six 4½" by fabric width strips dark coordinating fabric. Subcut a strip into one 4½" x 20" E strip and one 4½" x 22" F strip. Repeat with a second strip to make a total of two each E and F strips. Join the remaining strips on the short ends to make a long strip; subcut the strip into two 4½" x 70" D strips.

2. Cut five 1¼" by fabric width strips light coordinating fabric. Subcut one strip into four 1¼" x 10½" C strips. Join the remaining strips on the short ends to make a long strip; subcut the strip into two 1¼" x 70" B strips.

3. Cut six 2¼" by fabric width strips light coordinating fabric for binding.

Completing the Bed Runner

1. Lay out the 5" precut A squares and join to make rows referring to Figure 1; press seams in adjoining rows in opposite directions.

Figure 1

2. Join the pieced rows as arranged to complete the pieced center as shown in Figure 2; press seams in one direction.

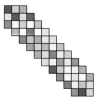

Figure 2

3. Trim each long side of the pieced center ¼" beyond seam intersections as shown in Figure 3 to complete the pieced center.

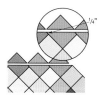

Figure 3

4. Fold and press each B and C strip in half with wrong sides together along length to make the flange strips.

5. With folded edge toward the pieced center, center and pin a B strip to opposite long sides of the pieced center and baste to hold in place as shown in Figure 4.

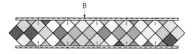

Figure 4

6. Trim excess B strips at each end using the angle of the pieced center as a guide for trimming as shown in Figure 5.

Figure 5

7. With folded edge toward the pieced center, place a C strip on the corner of one end of the pieced center and baste to hold in place as shown in Figure 6. Trim ends as in step 6.

Figure 6

8. Repeat step 7 with a second C strip on the same end referring to Figure 7.

Figure 7

9. Repeat steps 7 and 8 on the opposite end of the pieced center referring to the Placement Diagram for positioning of strips.

10. Center and sew a D strip to opposite sides of the pieced center; press seams toward D.

11. Trim ends of D strip to continue the angle of the pieced center as shown in Figure 8.

Figure 8

12. Sew an E strip to one end of the pieced center; press seam toward E and trim as for the D strips in step 11 and referring to Figure 9.

Figure 9

13. Repeat step 12 with an F strip on the same end and then with remaining E and F strips on the opposite end referring to Figure 10 to complete the pieced top.

Figure 10

14. Layer, quilt and bind referring to Finishing Your Quilt on page 160. ■

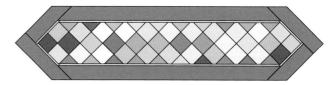

Forever Spring Bed Runner
Placement Diagram 87³/₄" x 20³/₄"

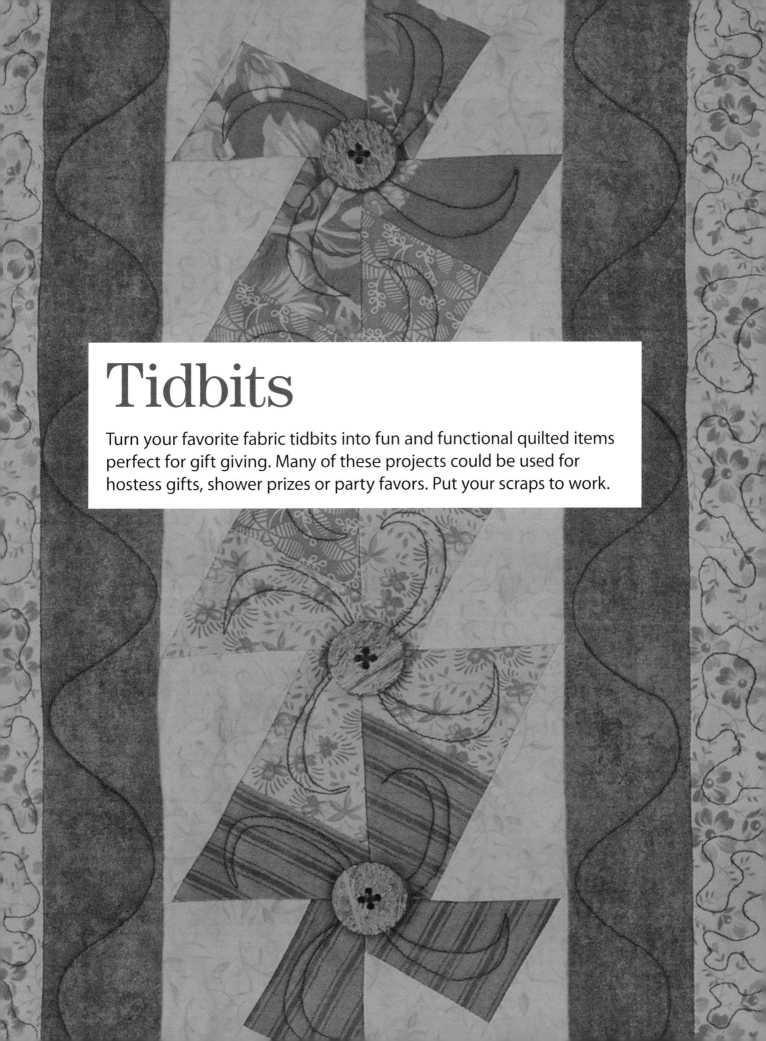

Tidbits

Turn your favorite fabric tidbits into fun and functional quilted items perfect for gift giving. Many of these projects could be used for hostess gifts, shower prizes or party favors. Put your scraps to work.

Free-Falling Leaves Dining Set

Capture the colors of the season. A dining set is the perfect way to dress up your table.

DESIGNS BY CHRIS MALONE

PROJECT SPECIFICATIONS

Skill Level: Beginner
Place Mat Size: 18" x 14½"
Napkin Holder Size: 1" x 9"
Block Size: 4½" x 4½"
Number of Blocks: 3 per place mat

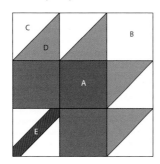

Maple Leaf
4¹/₂" x 4¹/₂" Block
Make 3

MATERIALS

Scrap green tonal
Assorted scraps 3 each red, purple and rust tonals
  or prints
1 fat quarter medium brown tonal
⅛ yard autumn print
⅛ yard cream tonal
Backing 19" x 16"
Batting 19" x 16" and 2" x 10"
Thread
Size 8 pearl cotton red, purple and rust
Embroidery needle
⅜" bias bar
Oak leaf button
Tracing paper
Basic sewing tools and supplies

Cutting

1. Cut three 1¼" x 3" green tonal E strips.

2. Cut three 2" A squares, two 2⅜" D squares and three 1½" I squares from each red, purple and rust scrap.

3. Cut one 13" x 14" F rectangle and one 1½" x 9½" J strip from medium brown tonal fat quarter.

4. Cut two 1" by fabric width autumn print strip; subcut into two each 1" x 18½" H and 1" x 14" G strips.

5. Cut one 2⅜" by fabric width cream tonal strip; subcut six each 2⅜" C and 2" B squares.

Completing the Blocks

1. Mark a diagonal line from corner to corner on the wrong side of each C square.

2. Place a C square right sides together with a D square; stitch ¼" on each side of the marked line as shown in Figure 1. Cut apart on the marked line and press with seam toward D to complete two C-D units, again referring to Figure 1.

Figure 1

3. Repeat step 2 with all C and D squares to complete four C-D units of each color.

4. Fold an E strip in half with wrong sides together along length; stitch along long raw edge. Trim seam allowance to ⅛".

5. Place bias bar inside the stitched E and move seam to the center of one side; press seam open to complete one stem piece. Remove bias bar. Repeat to make three stem pieces.

6. Center a stem piece on the diagonal of the right side of a B square and hand-stitch in place along both long sides as shown in Figure 2. Repeat to make three B/stem units. Trim ends of stems even with B squares.

Figure 2

7. To complete one Maple Leaf block, select same color-family A squares and C-D units. Sew an A square between a C-D and B/stem unit to make a stem row as shown in Figure 3; press seams toward A.

Figure 3

8. Join two A squares with one C-D unit to make a row as shown in Figure 4; press seams away from the center A square.

Figure 4

9. Join two C-D units with one B square to make a row as shown in Figure 5; press seams toward the center C-D unit.

Figure 5

10. Join the pieced rows referring to the block drawing to complete one Maple Leaf block; press seams in one direction.

11. Repeat steps 7–10 to complete a total of three Maple Leaf blocks.

Completing the Place Mat

1. Measure and mark a 9" square 2", and an 8" square 2½", in from the top and bottom edges of F as shown in Figure 6.

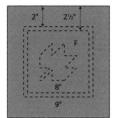

Figure 6

2. Trace the leaf shape from one of the blocks onto tracing paper; transfer the leaf shape to the center of the marked-squares area of F, again referring to Figure 6.

3. Arrange and join the three Maple Leaf blocks to make a strip as shown in Figure 7; press seams in one direction.

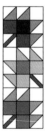

Figure 7

4. Sew the pieced strip to the marked F rectangle; press seams toward F.

5. Sew the G strips to opposite ends and the H strips to the top and bottom of the pieced center to complete the top.

6. Place the batting rectangle on a flat surface with the backing rectangle right side up on top; place the pieced top right sides together with the backing, aligning edges. Sew all around, leaving a 4" opening on one side. Clip corners, trim batting close to seam and turn right side out through the opening. Press edges flat.

7. Quilt on marked lines and in the ditch of seams.

8. Hand-quilt leaf veins in each leaf unit using an embroidery needle and 1 strand of pearl cotton to match the colors of blocks as shown in Figure 8 to finish.

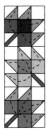

Figure 8

Completing the Napkin Holder

1. Place an I square right side up on the 2" x 10" batting strip; place a different-color I square right sides together with the I/batting layer and stitch as shown in Figure 9; press upper I to the right side.

Figure 9

2. Continue adding I squares to the batting strip in the same manner until the strip is covered. Trim batting even with I strip.

3. Place the I/batting strip right sides together with J and stitch all around leaving a 3" opening on one long side. Clip corners and batting close to seam. Turn right side out through the opening; press flat. Hand-stitch opening closed.

4. Machine-quilt ¼" from quilted strip edge all around.

5. Fold the quilted strip to make a loop as shown in Figure 10. Hand-stitch the button to attach layers at the second I on each strip end to complete the napkin holder. ■

Figure 10

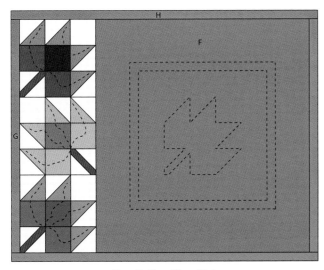

Free-Falling Place Mat
Placement Diagram 18" x 14¹/₂"

Napkin Holder
Placement Diagram 1" x 9"

Twist 'n' Spin Place Mats

Take a spin with a set of charm squares. The Lil' Twister tool makes these mats super simple—just in time for supper.

DESIGN BY TRICIA LYNN MALONEY

PROJECT SPECIFICATIONS

Skill Level: Beginner
Place Mat Size: 21¼" x 13¾"
Number of Place Mats: 2

MATERIALS

8 coordinating 5" A squares
½ yard tan tonal
½ yard brown tonal
⅝ yard green print
Backing 2 (25" x 18") pieces
Batting 2 (25" x 18") pieces
Thread
Lil' Twister ruler by CS Designs
8 (⅞") buttons (optional)
Basic sewing tools and supplies

Cutting

1. Cut four 3" by fabric width tan tonal strips; subcut four each 3" x 23½" B and 3" x 5" C strips.

2. Cut two 2" by fabric width brown tonal strips; subcut four 2" x 14¼" D strips.

3. Cut four 2¼" by fabric width brown tonal strips for binding.

4. Cut one 3½" by fabric width green print strip; subcut two 3½" x 14¼" E strips.

5. Cut one 11" by fabric width green print strip; subcut two 11" x 14¼" F rectangles.

Completing the Pieced Units

1. Select four A squares for one place mat.

2. Join the A squares to make an A strip as shown in Figure 1; press seams in one direction.

Figure 1

3. Sew a C strip to each short end and B strips to opposite long sides of the pieced A strip as shown in Figure 2; press seams toward B and C strips.

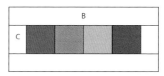

Figure 2

4. Place the Lil' Twister tool at the top left corner of the A-B-C strip with lines on the ruler aligned with the seam lines as shown in Figure 3; cut to make one pinwheel unit as shown in Figure 4. ***Note:*** *Using a rotating mat makes it easy to cut around all four sides of the ruler without moving the stitched unit or your body.*

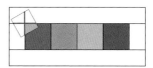

Figure 3

Figure 4

5. Moving left to right and top to bottom, position the tool on the seam lines and cut a total of 10 pinwheel units as shown in Figure 5. **Note:** *Handle and press the pinwheel units carefully. The edges are bias and will stretch easily.*

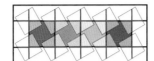

Figure 5

6. Lay out the pinwheel units in the same order they were cut to make two rows of five pinwheel units each as shown in Figure 6.

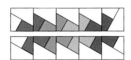

Figure 6

7. Join the pinwheel units as arranged to make two rows of five units each; press seams in opposite directions.

8. Join the two rows to complete the pinwheel strip as shown in Figure 7; press seam in one direction.

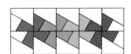

Figure 7

9. Trim the pinwheel strip ¼" away from the tips of the A fabrics to make a 5¼" x 14¼" strip as shown in Figure 8. Stitch ⅛" from the edge all around to stabilize the edges.

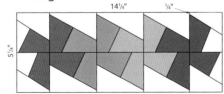

Figure 8

10. Repeat steps 1–9 to complete a second pinwheel strip.

Completing the Place Mats

1. Sew a D strip to opposite long sides of each pinwheel strip; press seams toward D strips.

2. Sew E to one D side and F to the other D side of the pieced strip to complete one place-mat top; press seams toward D strips.

3. Repeat step 2 with the second pieced strip, and E and F pieces, to complete a second place-mat top.

4. Sandwich one batting rectangle between one pieced top and one backing rectangle; pin or baste layers together to hold.

5. Quilt as desired by hand or machine; remove pins or basting. Trim excess backing and batting even with quilt top.

6. Join binding strips on short ends with diagonal seams to make one long strip; trim seams to ¼" and press seams open. Fold the strip in half along length with wrong sides together; press.

7. Sew binding to the right side of the place mat edges, overlapping ends. Fold binding to the back side and stitch in place.

8. Sew a button to the center of each pinwheel motif, if desired.

9. Repeat steps 4–8 to complete a second place mat. ■

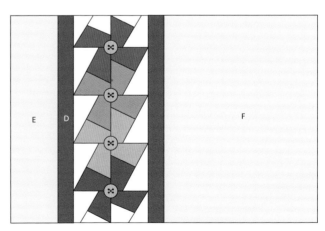

Twist 'n' Spin Place Mat
Placement Diagram 21¼" x 13¾"

Green Tea Place Mats & Hot Pads

Add a fresh, crisp look to your table with leftover strips, or purchase a precut package to liven up a table setting.

DESIGNS BY CONNIE KAUFFMAN

PROJECT SPECIFICATIONS

Skill Level: Beginner
Place Mat Size: 15" x 12"
Hot Pad Size: 7½" x 7½"

MATERIALS

Materials given are sufficient to complete two place mats and two hot pads.

Assorted batik scraps or 13–15 (2½" by width of fabric) strips coordinating batiks
1 fat eighth yellow tonal
1 yard backing fabric
Batting 2 (18" x 15") rectangles for place mats; 2 (9") squares for hot pads
2 (9") squares insulated batting for hot pads
Thread
Basic sewing tools and supplies

Cutting

1. Refer to the instructions and Figures 1 and 2 for sizes and colors to cut strips for place mats and hot pads from batik scraps or strips.

2. Cut 2¼"-wide batik strips to make a total length of 205" when joined to make binding for all projects.

3. Cut 4 (1½" x 2¼") rectangles yellow tonal for place mats.

4. Cut 2 (1½" x 1¾") rectangles yellow tonal for hot pads.

5. Cut 2 (19" x 16") backing rectangles for place mats.

6. Cut 2 (10") backing squares for hot pads.

Completing the Place Mats

1. Before cutting strips for one place mat, lay out the fabrics in a pleasing arrangement using two fabrics per row for 10 rows. Refer to Figure 1 for cut sizes of each piece, laying each piece in place as cut to maintain the chosen arrangement, inserting the yellow tonal rectangles with the mix as shown in Figure 1 for positioning.

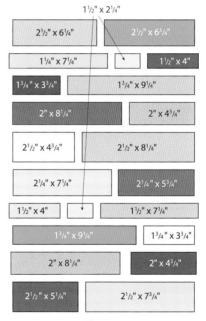

Figure 1

2. Select the two strips for row 1 and join on the short ends; press. Repeat with each row, place strips back in the arranged order as you stitch.

3. Join the rows as arranged to complete one place mat; press.

4. Layer, quilt and bind referring to Finishing Your Quilt on page 160.

5. Repeat all steps to complete a second place mat.

Completing the Hot Pads

1. Repeat all steps for Completing the Place Mats, except refer to Figure 2 for sizes to cut pieces and layer a square of the insulated batting in addition to the regular batting to finish two hot pads. **Note:** *Be sure to position the shiny side of the insulated batting toward the heat source.* ■

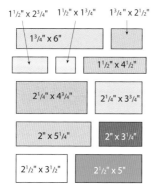

Figure 2

Designer's Tip

These place mats and hot pads provide the perfect projects for using up scraps. Sometimes scrap projects don't seem to coordinate, so select one fabric that can be used in several places and will stand out to tie everything together. The yellow tonal is used in each of these projects. As small as this little bit of color is in each place mat and hot pad, it is the perfect formula to send the message that this is a matching set.

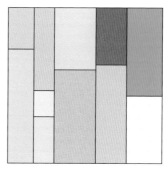

Green Tea Hot Pad
Placement Diagram 7½" x 7½"

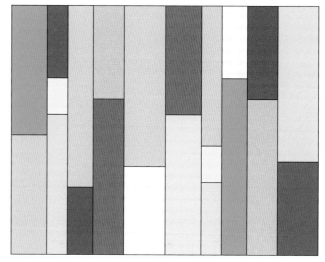

Green Tea Place Mat
Placement Diagram 15" x 12"

Autumn Ties Table Mat

Add a touch of color to any table with this handsome topper.

DESIGN BY CONNIE KAUFFMAN

PROJECT SPECIFICATIONS

Skill Level: Intermediate
Mat Size: 17" x 17" without prairie points

MATERIALS

1 fat quarter each 8 plaids in oranges, browns and rust
¼ yard green plaid
¾ yard brown/rust plaid (includes backing)
Batting 17½" x 17½"
Thread
12 assorted ⅞" brown buttons
Basic sewing tools and supplies

Cutting

1. Cut 2 (1½") B squares and 2 (2¾") C squares from each of the 8 plaids (16 total of each size).

2. Cut 1 (3¼" x 21") strip each plaid. Subcut each strip into 3 (3¼") F squares (24 total).

3. Cut 2 (2¾" by fabric width) green plaid strips; subcut strips into 20 (2¾") A squares.

4. Cut 2 (2¼" by fabric width) brown/rust plaid strips; subcut strips into 4 (2¼" x 9½") E strips and 4 (1¾" x 7") D strips.

5. Cut 1 (17½" x 17½") brown/rust plaid backing piece.

Completing Pieced Center

1. Mark a diagonal line from corner to corner on the wrong side of each B square.

2. Arrange five A squares with two pairs of matching C squares in three rows of three squares each as shown in Figure 1.

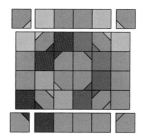

Figure 1

3. Select two B squares to match each of the C squares and arrange right sides together on the A squares as shown in Figure 2.

Figure 2

4. Select and stitch one B square to A on the marked line as arranged referring to Figure 3; press B to the right side. Repeat with remaining selected B pieces on A squares, referring again to Figures 2 and 3.

Figure 3

5. Repeat steps 2–4 with remaining A, B and C squares.

6. Arrange and join the pieced units and plain A and C squares as arranged, leaving the top and bottom rows and each A-B corner unit unattached to the center unit as shown in Figure 4.

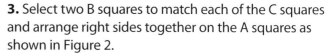

Figure 4

Completing the Quilt

1. Measure 1" from the A/B seam line on the unattached A-B units and mark a diagonal line as shown in Figure 5. Trim on the line.

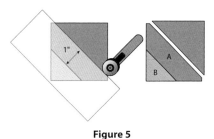

Figure 5

2. Center and sew a D strip to each trimmed A-B corner, press seams toward D. Trim strip even with the edges of the A-B corner as shown in Figure 6.

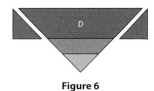

Figure 6

3. Sew an E strip to the top and bottom rows as shown in Figure 7. Sew an E strip to each side of the center unit. Press seams toward E.

Figure 7

4. Sew a corner unit to each end of each of the top and bottom rows as shown in Figure 8.

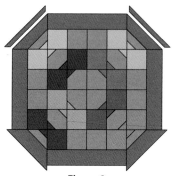

Figure 8

5. Sew these rows to the center unit and trim excess D strip even with the E strips, again referring to Figure 8.

6. Fold each F square with wrong sides together on one diagonal; fold again on the diagonal to make a prairie point referring to Figure 9.

Figure 9

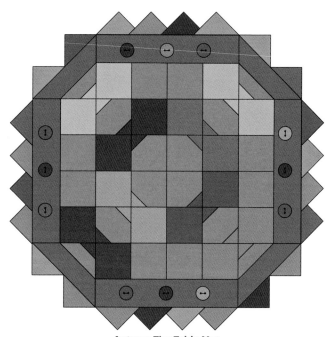

Autumn Ties Table Mat
Placement Diagram 17" x 17" without prairie points

7. Arrange four prairie points on each E strip and two on each corner unit, aligning long edges with the edges of the pieced top (points toward the center) referring to Figure 10. Baste to hold in place. **Note:** *Make sure the folds of the prairie points face in the same direction so the adjacent prairie points can slip inside each other to adjust to fit. Corner prairie points may not overlap.*

Figure 10

8. Place the backing and pieced top right sides together on top of the batting square; pin around outer edges. Sew all around, leaving a 3" opening on one side for turning.

9. Turn right side out through the opening and press prairie points out. Turn opening edges to the inside and hand-stitch closed.

10. Quilt as desired.

11. Evenly space and sew three buttons to the center of each E strip to finish. ■

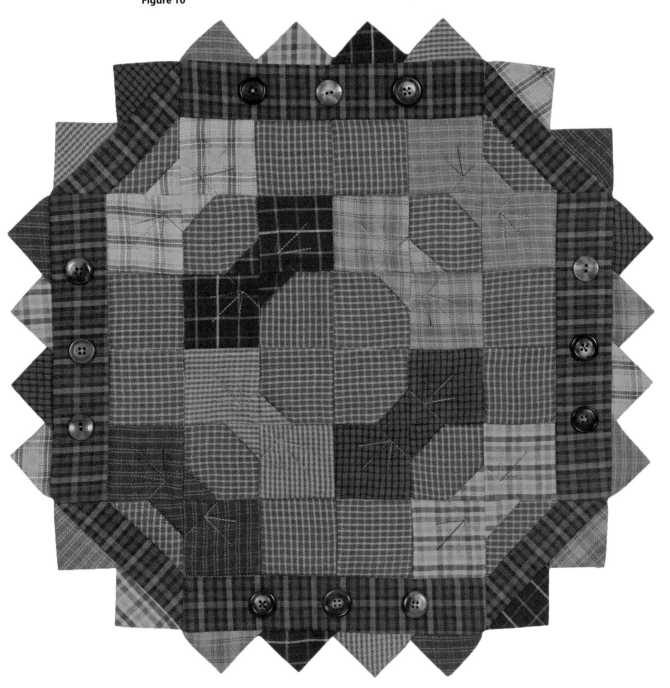

Scrappy Heart Candle Mat

A simple tool makes short work of creating the heart-shaped yo-yos used on the edge of this valentine candle mat.

DESIGN BY ROCHELLE MARTIN OF COTTAGE QUILT DESIGNS

PROJECT SPECIFICATIONS

Skill Level: Beginner
Mat Size: 14" x 14" with yo-yos

MATERIALS

Assorted pink print scraps
Assorted medium and dark red print scraps
Backing 12½" x 12½"
Batting 12½" x 12½"
Thread
Clover Small Heart-Shaped Quick Yo-Yo Maker
Basic sewing tools and supplies

Cutting

1. Cut a total of 24 (3½") pink print scrap A squares.

2. Cut a total of 24 (3½") medium and dark red print scrap B squares.

Completing the Yo-Yos

1. Center an A square over the back of the yo-yo maker disk, with the wrong side of the square against the disk back.

2. Insert the disk into the plate and snap securely in place as shown in Photo 1.

Photo 1

3. Trim away the excess fabric around the disk leaving a ⅛"–³⁄₁₆" seam allowance; slash the seam allowance in the valley of the heart through the slash mark in the back plate as shown in Photo 2.

Photo 2

4. Thread a needle with thread to match the square; knot one end. Fold the seam allowance down against the front of the disk; insert the needle at the starting point down through the disk and back up through the hole at the other end of the slot on the back of the plate as shown in Photo 3.

Photo 3

5. Continue to stitch down and then back up at each end of each slot.

6. At the valley of the heart, make sure the seam allowance is spread apart as you sew through the two vertical slots as shown in Photo 4 on page 130; continue sewing around the rest of the disk and along

the starting slot again bringing the needle to the disk side to end as shown in Photo 5.

7. Push the disk out of the plate; hold the edge of the fabric heart with your fingers and pull the disk out of the fabric.

8. Pull the thread to gather the fabric and evenly distribute it around the yo-yo shape, turning the seam allowance in; shape the heart yo-yo by pulling out the tops of the heart and folding in the fabric at the valley of the heart.

9. Pull the thread to make a heart shape; knot the thread. Hide the thread end by inserting the needle into the opening and exiting through the yo-yo as shown in Photo 6. Clip the thread.

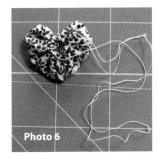

10. Repeat all steps to complete 16 each A and B yo-yo hearts.

Completing the Topper

1. Arrange and join two each A and B squares to make two each A-B and B-A rows of four units each as shown in Figure 1; press seams toward B.

Figure 1

2. Arrange and join the rows, alternating the A-B and B-A rows to complete the pieced top referring to the Placement Diagram for positioning; press seams in one direction.

3. Lay the pieced top right side up on the batting square; trim edges even. Lay the backing square right sides together with the layered top and batting; pin to hold. Stitch all around edges, leaving a 4" opening on one side; turn right side out through opening.

4. Press seams of opening ¼" to the inside; hand-stitch opening closed.

5. Quilt as desired by hand or machine.

6. Evenly space and pin one each A and B yo-yo heart to the edge of each A and B square referring to the Placement Diagram for positioning and color placement; hand-stitch edges of yo-yo hearts in place at edges from the back side with thread to match fabrics to complete the candle mat. ■

Scrappy Heart Candle Mat
Placement Diagram 14" x 14" with yo-yo hearts

Selvage Backpack

This is a great back-to-school project. Any student, young or old, would love to carry their books in this backpack.

DESIGN BY CHRISTINE A. SCHULTZ

PROJECT SPECIFICATIONS

Skill Level: Confident Beginner
Backpack Size: Approximately 10½" x 14½" x 4"

MATERIALS

4" square scrap print
10" square scrap lining
75 selvage strips
⅞ yard red print lining
Batting: 2 (16" x 18") rectangles, 1 (9" x 11") rectangle
Thread
1½ yards coordinating cotton strapping
1 (1⅛") coordinating button
1 small button for inside
24" length ¼" cotton cord
2 parachute buckles
1⅛ yards 1"-wide coordinating grosgrain ribbon
1 spring-type cord stop
1 yard red rattail or other cord
Sewing machine feet suggested:
　　Zipper foot
　　Machine quilting foot
Basic sewing tools and supplies

Cutting

1. Cut one 3" triangle from scrap print.

2. Cut 8" square for pocket lining from scrap lining.

3. Cut 75 (1¼" x 18") selvage strips.

4. From the red print lining, cut two 15" x 17" rectangles, one 1¼" x 5" strip, one 8" x 10" flap rectangle, one 8" pocket square and one 1¾" x 24" bias strip for piping.

Completing the Piecing

1. Position batting on flat surface with the 16" edges as the width. Draw lines through the horizontal center of each 16" x 18" batting rectangle; draw two more lines dividing each half of each piece in half again. These lines will serve as guidelines for placement to keep selvage strips straight.

2. Lay a selvage strip right side up with finished edge down toward the bottom edge of one of the marked batting rectangles. Lay a second selvage strip over the first strip and pin in place so the finished edge overlaps the raw edge of the previous strip about ¼" as shown in Figure 1. **Note:** *The ends of the selvage strips should extend past the edges of batting at each side edge.*

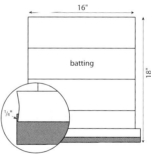

Figure 1

3. Using a machine quilting foot, topstitch close to overlapped edges as shown in Figure 2.

Figure 2

4. Continue adding selvage strips to the batting in the same manner until the batting is covered with strips, using the drawn lines as guides to keep strips straight.

5. Machine-quilt vertical lines from top to bottom as desired to add texture; press.

6. Repeat steps 2–5 to cover the second marked batting rectangle with selvage strips.

7. Trim the two stitched units to 15" x 17" for the outer backpack pieces.

8. Using the 9" x 11" batting rectangle for the flap piece, begin by centering the 3" triangle at the top edge of the batting as shown in Figure 3.

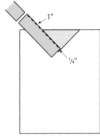

Figure 3   **Figure 4**

9. Lay the first selvage strip with the finished edge over one short side of the triangle, overlapping ¼", as shown in Figure 4. Topstitch close to overlapped edges, again referring to Figure 4. Trim end of strip, leaving approximately 1" extending beyond the batting.

10. Lay a second selvage strip with finished edge over the other short side of the triangle, overlapping the edge of the triangle and the end of the previous selvage strip as shown in Figure 5; topstitch in place close to overlapped edges, again referring to Figure 5. Trim end of strip.

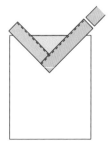

Figure 5

11. Continue placing and topstitching selvage strips in this manner, alternating sides, until the batting is covered as shown in Figure 6.

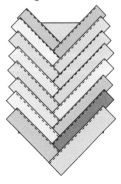

Figure 6

12. Make a flap pattern using the pattern given. Use the pattern to trim the batting to size as shown in Figure 7.

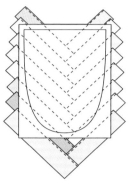

Figure 7

Completing the Backpack

1. Place the two trimmed outer backpack rectangles right sides together, matching edges; join along one long edge using a ¼" seam allowance.

2. Cut 14 (2½") lengths grosgrain ribbon; fold each length in half to make 1¼"-long loops; machine-baste raw edges of loops to hold as shown in Figure 8.

Figure 8

3. Evenly space and pin the basted loops along the top raw edge of the stitched backpack rectangles, leaving 7½" without loops on one edge as shown in Figure 9; baste in place.

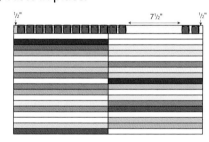

Figure 9

4. Cut one 8", two 4" and two 24" lengths cotton strapping. Slide each 4"-long piece through one end of the parachute buckles as shown in Figure 10.

Figure 10

5. Baste the strap/half buckles in place at the bottom edge of the back backpack rectangle 4" in from the side seam and 4¼" in from the raw side edge as shown in Figure 11.

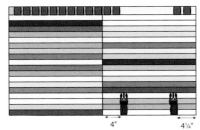

Figure 11

6. Baste the 24"-long pieces of cotton strapping in place at the top edge of the back of the backpack, 4" from seam line and 4¼" in from the raw side edge as shown in Figure 12. Baste the 8"-long handle piece of cotton strapping ¼" inside the strap pieces, again referring to Figure 12.

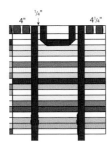

Figure 12

7. With right side down, fold the two long edges of the 1¼" x 5" strip red print to the center, then fold in half and press as shown in Figure 13.

Figure 13

8. Fold the strip in half again and zigzag along open edge. Cut in half. Fold each piece in half to make a front button loop and a key tab. Set the button loop aside.

9. Baste the key tab in place along the open side seam about 4" down from the top edge of backpack front as shown in Figure 14.

Figure 14

10. Fold the outer backpack with right sides together aligning the side seams; stitch side seam and bottom

edge. Stitch over the seam a second time to secure; press seams open.

11. Draw a line 2" up each side seam from bottom seam; fold each corner to match the bottom and side seams to make a point; stitch along the 2" marks to make square corners as shown in Figure 15; stitch along the stitched line a second time to secure.

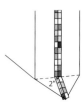

Figure 15

12. Fold the corners to the bottom and hand-stitch in place to hold flat; set aside.

13. Layer the 8" x 8" scrap pocket lining square with the 8" x 8" red print pocket square wrong sides together. Cut a 9"-long selvage strip and place on the lining side with right sides and raw edges together; stitch as shown in Figure 16.

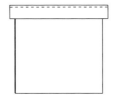

Figure 16

Figure 17

14. Press the selvage strip to the red print side and over the top edge of the layered pocket/lining squares; topstitch in place through both layers as shown in Figure 17. Trim strip ends even with the pocket square.

15. Turn the raw edges of the pocket ¼" to the lining side; press and baste to hold.

16. Center and stitch the pocket in place on the right side of 15" x 17" back lining piece down 4" from the top edge, securing top edge corners as shown in Figure 18.

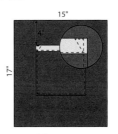

Figure 18

Figure 19

17. Place the front and back lining pieces right sides together and stitch sides and along bottom, leaving a 4" opening in one side seam as shown in Figure 19.

18. Repeat steps 11 and 12 to make square bottom corners in the lining; press lining seams flat.

19. Lay cotton cord in the center of the wrong side of the 1¾" x 24" bias strip for piping. Fold strip over cord to enclose, matching raw edges.

20. Using a zipper foot, stitch close to cord through all layers to make piping for the flap; trim seam allowance to ¼" as shown in Figure 20.

Figure 20

21. Lay the piping along the right-side edge of the flap with raw edges even; stitch just outside the previous stitching line using a zipper foot.

22. Fold the button loop made in steps 7 and 8 in half and baste in place at the center front of the right side of the flap with raw edges aligned as shown in Figure 21.

 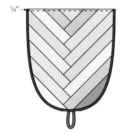

Figure 21   **Figure 22**

23. Pin the flap right sides together with the 8" x 10" lining rectangle; machine-stitch on the batting side, just outside the previous stitching line, leaving top edge open. Trim lining even with the flap and turn right side out; steam-press. Machine-baste straight edge closed ¼" from edge as shown in Figure 22.

24. With right sides together and aligning the center of the flap and the back of the backpack, baste the prepared flap to the top edge of the back of the outer bag as shown in Figure 23. **Note:** *The flap will be on top of the basted strapping.*

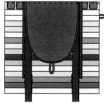

Figure 23

Selvage Backpack Back
Placement Diagram 10½" x 14½" x 4"

Selvage Backpack Front
Placement Diagram 10½" x 14½" x 4"

25. Cut two 15" lengths of rattail cord; baste cord ends to top edge of backpack at sides of flap, again referring to Figure 23 on page 135.

26. Turn the backpack, shell wrong side out and lining right side out; slide the lining inside the outer backpack with right sides together; pin top edges together, aligning side seams as shown in Figure 24.

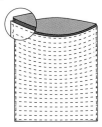

Figure 24

27. Stitch all the way around the top edge of the backpack, being careful to slow down at bulky areas so as not to break the needle.

28. Turn the backpack right side out through the opening in the side of the lining seam; hand-stitch opening closed. Press top edge to make a neat fold. Topstitch ¼" away from the top folded edge.

29. Lace the rattail cords through the ribbon tabs, working from back to center front, and add cord stop; knot ends of cords.

30. Following manufacturer's instructions, lace 24" cotton strapping pieces through the outer half of the parachute buckles so they are adjustable but secure.

31. To finish, fold the flap over and mark button position in the center of the front of the backpack. Sew buttons in place back to back, with the larger button on the outside and the smaller one on the inside for strength. ▮

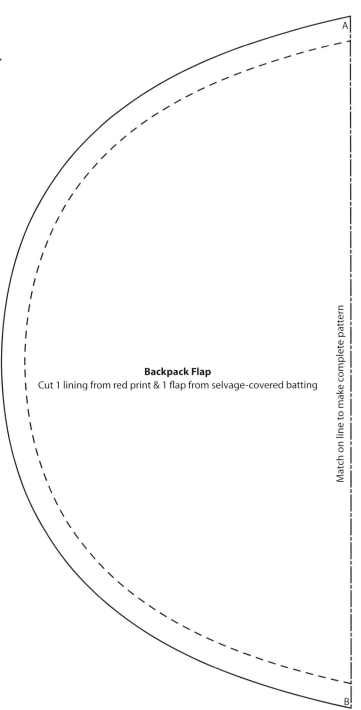

A

Backpack Flap
Cut 1 lining from red print & 1 flap from selvage-covered batting

Match on line to make complete pattern

B

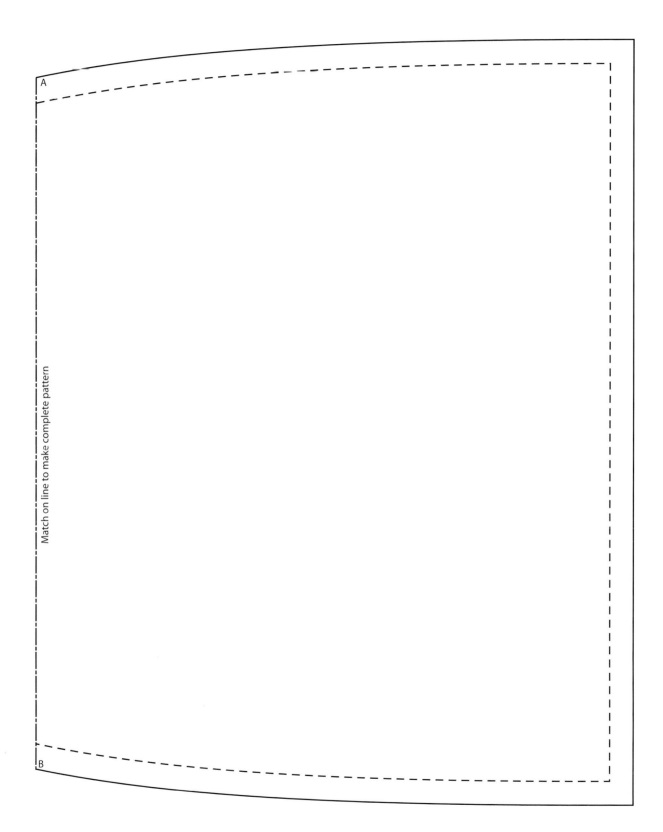

A

B

Match on line to make complete pattern

County Fair Trio

Showcase your skills without making a large quilt. The block, with its flying-geese units and hourglass patches, provides enough interest and challenge to make once, twice, three times!

DESIGN BY GINA GEMPESAW
QUILTED BY CAROLE WHALING

PROJECT SPECIFICATIONS

Skill Level: Intermediate
Pillow Size: 18" x 18"

PROJECT NOTE

The pieced pillow units are all made using the same size/lettered pieces. Note how different the three projects look using the different colors.

MATERIALS

¼ yard yellow/green batik
¼ yard dark red batik
⅓ yard dark blue batik
⅜ yard medium blue batik
1¾ yards red/blue print batik
2 yards red print multicolored batik
2⅛ yards light teal batik
3 (18½") batting squares
Thread
3 (18") square pillow forms
Basic sewing tools and supplies

Cutting

1. Cut one 4¼" by fabric width yellow/green batik strip. Subcut into one 4¼" square; cut on both diagonals to make four D2 triangles.

2. From remainder of strip, cut four 2⅜" squares. Cut each square in half on one diagonal to make eight C2 triangles.

3. Cut one 4¼" by fabric width dark red batik strip. Subcut into three 4¼" squares; cut on both diagonals to make eight F1 and four D3 triangles.

4. From remainder of strip, cut four each 2" E1 squares and 2⅜" squares. Cut each 2⅜" square in half on one diagonal to make eight C3 triangles.

5. Cut one 4¼" by fabric width dark blue batik strip. Subcut five 4¼" squares; cut each square on both diagonals to make four D1 and eight each F2 and F3 triangles.

6. From remainder of strip, cut four 2⅜" squares. Cut each square in half on one diagonal to make eight C1 triangles.

7. Cut one 2" by fabric width dark blue batik strip; subcut into four each E2 and E3 2" squares.

8. Cut one 4¼" by fabric width medium blue batik strip. Subcut eight 4¼" squares; cut each square on both diagonals to make eight B1 and 12 each G2 and G3 triangles.

9. Cut one 3½" by fabric width medium blue batik strip. Subcut one each 3½" A2 and A3 square.

10. From remainder of strip, cut 12 (2⅜") squares. Cut each square in half on one diagonal to make 24 H1 triangles.

11. Cut one 5" by fabric width red/blue print batik strip; subcut four 5" J3 squares and eight 2" K3 squares.

12. Cut two 2" by fabric width red/blue print batik strips; subcut two each 2" x 15½" L3 strips and 2" x 18½" M3 strips.

13. Cut one 22" by fabric width red/blue print batik strip; subcut one 22" backing square.

14. Cut one 26" by fabric width red/blue print batik strip; subcut two 18½" pillow back squares.

15. Cut one 4¼" by fabric width red print multicolored batik strip; subcut two 4¼" squares. Cut each square on both diagonals to make eight B2 triangles.

16. From remainder of strip, cut 12 (2⅜") squares. Subcut each square in half on one diagonal to make 24 H2 triangles.

17. Cut one 5" by fabric width red print multicolored batik strip; subcut four 5" J1 squares and eight 2" K1 squares.

18. Cut two 2" by fabric width red print multicolored batik strips; subcut two each 2" x 15½" L1 strips and 2" x 18½" M1 strips.

19. Cut one 22" by fabric width red print multicolored batik strip; subcut one 22" backing square.

20. Cut one 26" by fabric width red print multicolored batik strip; subcut two 18½" pillow back squares.

21. Cut one 4¼" by fabric width light teal batik strip; subcut five 4¼" squares. Cut each square on both diagonals to make 12 G1 and eight B3 triangles.

22. Cut one 3½" by fabric width light teal batik strip; subcut one 3½" A1.

23. From remainder of strip, cut 12 (2⅜") squares. Subcut each square in half on one diagonal to make 24 H3 triangles.

24. Cut one 5" by fabric width light teal batik strip; subcut four 5" J2 squares and eight 2" K2 squares.

25. Cut two 2" by fabric width light teal batik strips; subcut two each 2" x 15½" L2 strips and 2" x 18½" M2 strips.

26. Cut one 22" by fabric width light teal batik strip; subcut one 22" backing square.

27. Cut one 26" by fabric width light teal batik strip; subcut two 18½" pillow back squares.

Completing the County Fair Piecing

1. Select all County Fair 1 lettered pieces (A1, B1, etc.).

2. Sew a C triangle to each short side of B to make a B-C unit as shown in Figure 1; press seams toward C. Repeat to make a total of four B-C units.

Figure 1

3. Sew an H triangle to each short side of G to make a G-H unit as shown in Figure 2; press seams toward H. Repeat to make a total of 12 G-H units.

Figure 2

4. Sew B to F and D to F as shown in Figure 3; press seams toward F. Join the pieced units to complete an F unit, again referring to Figure 3; press seam to one side. Repeat to make a total of four F units.

Figure 3

5. Sew a B-C unit to the D side and a G-H unit to the B side of an F unit to complete a side unit as shown in Figure 4; press seams toward the F unit. Repeat to make a total of four side units.

Figure 4

6. Sew K to a G-H unit and add to J as shown in Figure 5; press seam toward K and then J.

Figure 5

7. Sew a K square to one end and an E square to the opposite end of a G-H unit as shown in Figure 6; press seams toward E and K.

Figure 6

8. Sew the unit made in step 7 to the unit made in step 6 to make a corner unit as shown in Figure 7; press seam toward the J square.

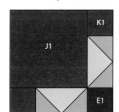

Figure 7

9. Repeat steps 6–8 to complete a total of four corner units.

10. Sew a side unit to opposite sides of A to complete the center row as shown in Figure 8; press seams toward A.

Figure 8

11. Sew a corner unit to opposite sides of each remaining side unit to complete the top and bottom rows referring to Figure 9; press seams toward the corner units.

Figure 9

12. Sew the center row between the top and bottom rows to complete the County Fair 1 unit referring to Figure 10; press seams toward the center row.

Figure 10

13. Repeat steps 1–12 with the County Fair 2 lettered pieces (A2, B2, etc.) to make the County Fair 2 unit referring to Figure 11, and with the County Fair 3 lettered pieces (A3, B3, etc.) to make the County Fair 3 unit referring to Figure 12.

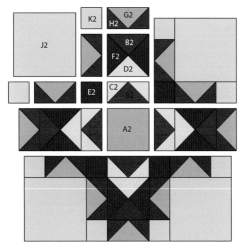

Figure 11

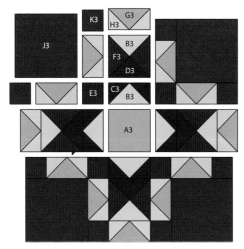

Figure 12

Completing the Pillows

1. Sew an L strip to top and bottom, and M strips to the remaining sides of each County Fair unit; press seams toward L and M strips.

2. Sandwich a batting square between a bordered unit and a 22" backing square; pin or baste to hold layers together.

3. Quilt each layered unit as desired by hand or machine. When quilting is complete, trim batting and backing edges even with pillow top edges. Remove pins or basting.

4. Fold each pillow back rectangle in half with wrong sides together to make six 18½" x 13" rectangles; press.

5. Place two pillow back rectangles on the right side of each pillow top, overlapping folded edges as shown in Figure 13; stitch all around.

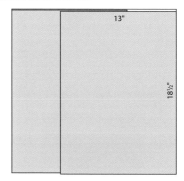

Figure 13

6. Clip corners; turn right side out. Press edges flat.

7. Insert a pillow form through back opening of each pillow to finish. ∎

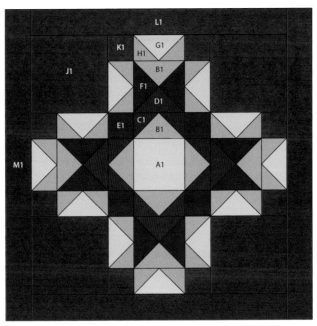

County Fair 1
Placement Diagram 18" x 18"

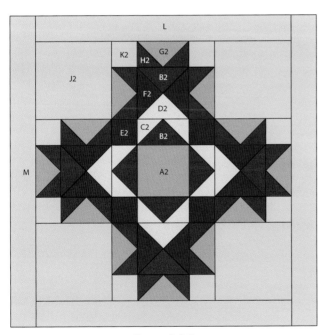

County Fair 2
Placement Diagram 18" x 18"

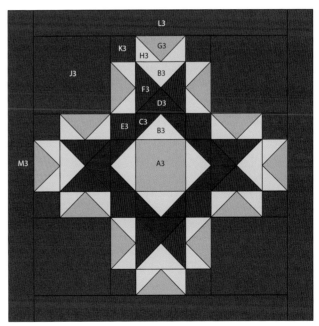

County Fair 3
Placement Diagram 18" x 18"

Bottle & Cup Wraps

Make one or make a dozen of these easy, colorful wraps. Now you can cover any disposable water bottle or drink cup in a quilted piece of sunshine.

DESIGNED & QUILTED BY GINA GEMPESAW

PROJECT SPECIFICATIONS

Skill Level: Beginner
Cup Wrap Size: 14" x 6"
Bottle Wrap Size: 10" x 6"

MATERIALS

1 fat eighth each gold and orange solids or tonals
1 fat eighth each green, red and teal solids or tonals
1 fat eighth multicolored circle print
⅝ yard multicolored print
Batting 16" x 8" and 12" x 8"
Neutral-color all-purpose thread
Quilting thread
½ yard hook-and-loop tape
Basic sewing tools and supplies

PROJECT NOTES

Your favorite beverage container may have slightly different dimensions than those used here. Measure the circumference of the container at the top and at the bottom, and then measure the height of the container. Add about 2" to each measurement to determine the size of the wrap you need if adjustments are necessary.

Cutting

1. Cut two 1½" x 21" strips each gold and orange solids or tonals. Subcut the gold strips into 24 (1½") C squares. Subcut the orange strips into 24 (1½") D squares.

2. Cut one 1½" x 21" strip from each green, red and teal solids or tonals. Subcut the green strip into 14 (1½") A squares. Subcut the red strip into 14 (1½") E squares. Subcut the teal strip into 10 (1½") G squares.

3. Cut two 1½" by fabric width multicolored circle print strips; subcut into 30 (1½") F squares.

4. Cut one 1½" x 21" multicolored print strip; subcut strip into 28 (1½") B squares.

5. Cut one 8" by fabric width multicolored print strip; subcut strip into one 12" x 8" backing and one 16" x 8" backing.

6. Cut three 2¼" by fabric width multicolored print strips for binding.

Completing the Cup Wrap

1. Arrange and join 14 each C and D squares with A, B and E squares in six rows of 14 squares each to form a diagonal pattern as shown in Figure 1. Press seams in adjoining rows in opposite directions.

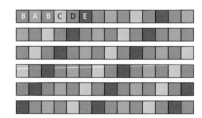

Figure 1

2. Join the rows to complete a pieced rectangle as shown in Figure 2; press seams in one direction. ***Note:*** *Check that your cup wrap will fit the cup for which it was designed. Adjust as necessary.*

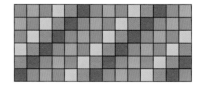

Figure 2

3. Sandwich the 16" x 8" batting between the 16" x 8" backing piece and the pieced cup-wrap top; quilt as desired by hand or machine.

4. When quilting is complete, trim batting and backing edges even with the pieced cup-wrap top.

5. To make the cup-wrap shape, trim from the top left corner to the seam between the bottom A and B squares using a straightedge and rotary cutter as shown in Figure 3. Repeat from the top right corner to the seam between the bottom D and E squares, again referring to Figure 3.

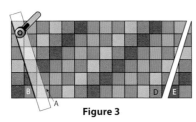

Figure 3

6. Join the binding strips with diagonal seams; cut strip into one 50" and one 44" length. Set aside the 44" length for the bottle wrap.

7. Fold and press the 50" binding strip with wrong sides together along length. Stitch the binding strip to the cup wrap matching raw edges, mitering corners and overlapping at the beginning and end.

8. Turn the binding to the inside; hand-stitch in place.

9. Cut a hook-and-loop strip 5¾" long, angling ends to match angle on the cup wrap. Pin the hook strip to the wrong side of the right end of the cup wrap as shown in Figure 4.

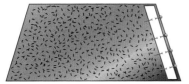

Figure 4

10. Pin the loop strip to the right side of the left end of the cup wrap as shown in Figure 5.

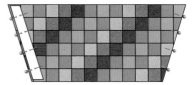

Figure 5

11. When satisfied with positioning, machine-stitch the hook and loop pieces in place to finish the cup wrap.

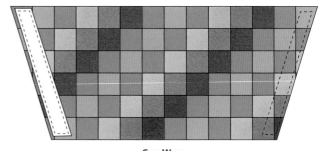

Cup Wrap
Placement Diagram 14" x 6"

Completing the Bottle Wrap

1. Arrange and join 10 each C and D squares with F and G squares in six rows of 10 squares each to form a diagonal pattern as shown in Figure 6. Press seams in adjoining rows in opposite directions.

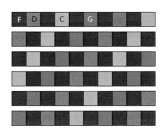

Figure 6

2. Join the rows to complete a pieced rectangle as shown in Figure 7; press seams in one direction. **Note:** *Check that the quilted bottle-wrap top will fit around your favorite-size bottle. Adjust as necessary.*

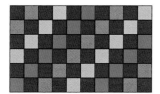

Figure 7

3. Sandwich the 12" x 8" batting between the 12" x 8" backing piece and the pieced bottle-wrap top; quilt as desired by hand or machine.

4. When quilting is complete, trim batting and backing edges even with the pieced bottle-wrap top.

5. Fold and press the 44" binding strip with wrong sides together along length. Stitch the binding strip to the bottle wrap matching raw edges, mitering corners and overlapping the beginning and end.

6. Turn the binding to the inside; hand-stitch in place.

7. Cut a hook-and-loop strip 5¼" long. Pin the hook strip to the wrong side of the right end of the bottle wrap as shown in Figure 8.

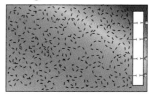

Figure 8

8. Pin the loop strip to the right side of the left end of the bottle wrap as shown in Figure 9.

Figure 9

9. When satisfied with positioning, machine-stitch the hook and loop pieces in place to finish the bottle wrap. ■

Bottle Wrap
Placement Diagram 10" x 6"

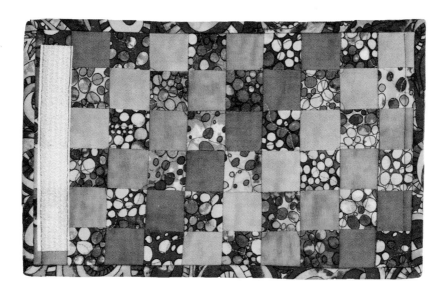

Clever Clutch

Turn your stash into valuable projects. This cute little clutch will store all your small quilting notions or makeup.

DESIGN BY LYNN WEGLARZ

PROJECT SPECIFICATIONS

Skill Level: Beginner
Clutch Size: Approximately 8½" x 6½"

MATERIALS

1 fat eighth white/orange print
1 fat quarter orange/red dot
1 fat quarter coordinating stripe
Thread
9" coordinating zipper
⅓ yard woven cotton fusible interfacing
⅝"–¾" button
Size 3 or 4 snap
Basic sewing tools and supplies

Cutting

1. Cut one 4½" x 9" white/orange print B rectangle.

2. Bond the cotton woven fusible interfacing to the wrong side of the orange/red dot. Cut two 7" x 9" A rectangles.

3. Prepare template for tab using pattern given; cut two orange/red dot tabs.

4. Cut one 2½" x 9" coordinating stripe C piece along bias and one 1" x 7" bias D strip for zipper pull.

5. Cut remaining coordinating stripe into 1¾"-wide bias strips to total 22" when joined.

Completing the Clutch

1. Place the two tab pieces right sides together, matching raw edges. Stitch around edges, leaving the short end open as shown in Figure 1.

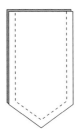

Figure 1

2. Clip corners and turn the stitched tab right side out; press flat.

3. Topstitch long and point edges of tab as shown in Figure 2.

Figure 2

4. Center and baste the tab to one A rectangle as shown in Figure 3 to make the clutch front.

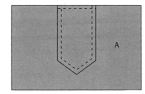

Figure 3

5. With right sides together, stitch C to one 9" edge of B as shown in Figure 4; press seam toward B.

Figure 4

6. Press the long edge of C ¼" to the wrong side. Press C to the wrong side to cover the B/C seam as shown in Figure 5; stitch in the ditch of the B/C seam to finish the pocket.

Figure 5

7. Place the pocket piece right side up on the clutch front under tab, matching bottom edges; baste in place around edges as shown in Figure 6.

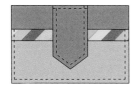

Figure 6

8. Referring to Figure 7 and using a zipper foot, stitch one side of the zipper tape to the right side of the top edge of the clutch front.

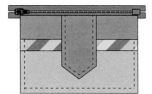

Figure 7

9. Repeat with the second side of the zipper tape on one 9" edge of the remaining A rectangle. Press A pieces away from the zipper tape; topstitch in place as shown in Figure 8.

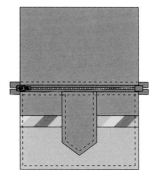

Figure 8

10. Unzip zipper halfway. With right sides together, matching side and bottom edges, stitch around edges using a big ¼" seam allowance to make the clutch as shown in Figure 9.

Figure 9

11. Press ¼" to the wrong side on one short end and one long side of the 22" stripe bias strip. Place pressed end at the top zipper edge of one side of the seam stitched in step 10, right side down, and referring to Figure 10, stitch the raw edge of the strip to the stitched seam, mitering at corners as shown in Figure 11.

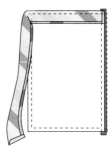

Figure 10

Figure 11

12. When you reach the opposite end, trim any excess ¼" beyond the end, fold the end to the wrong side and complete the seam.

13. Press the bias strip to the right side to enclose the seam and topstitch in place from the inside to finish the seam as shown in Figure 12.

Figure 12

14. Match one bottom and side seam and draw a line 1½" from the point as shown in Figure 13; stitch on the marked line to make a square corner. Repeat to make the second square corner.

Figure 13

15. Tack the corner points to the side seams referring to Figure 14. Turn right side out.

Figure 14

16. Referring to Figure 15, fold each long raw edge of the D strip to the center and press; fold in half and stitch along the open edge to make the zipper pull. Cut each end at an angle. Thread one end through the zipper tab and tie a knot to hold.

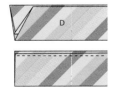

Figure 15

17. Sew the button 1" from the point of the tab. Add the snap pieces to the wrong side of the tab and to the pocket to finish. ■

Clever Clutch Bag
Placement Diagram Approximately 8½" x 6½"

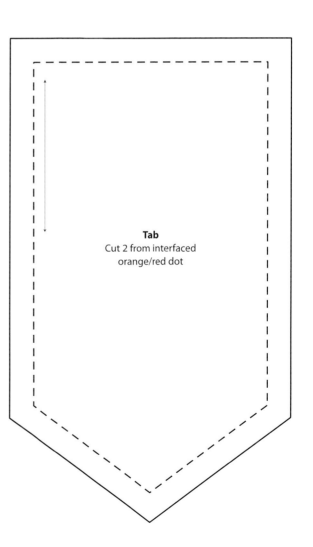

Tab
Cut 2 from interfaced
orange/red dot

Card Keeper & Matching Cards

Never miss sending a card for a special event again. This cute card keeper is the perfect way to organize cards and use scraps.

DESIGN BY TRICIA LYNN MALONEY

PROJECT SPECIFICATIONS

Skill Level: Beginner
Keeper Size: Approximately 8" x 6½"

CARD KEEPER

MATERIALS

1 fat quarter focus fabric
¼ yard total assorted coordinating scraps to match focus fabric
Batting 8½" x 18½"
Thread
2" length of coordinating rickrack
Coordinating button
Basic sewing tools and supplies

Cutting

1. Cut one 8½" x 18½" focus fabric lining rectangle.

2. Cut three focus fabric A strips 8½" long in various widths.

3. Cut 8–12 assorted 8½"-long assorted coordinating scrap B strips in varying widths.

Completing Card Keeper

1. Arrange and join the assorted A and B strips on the 8½" edges to make a long pieced strip.

2. Trim pieced strip to 8½" x 18½" for the card keeper top as shown in Figure 1.

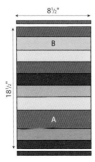

Figure 1

3. Measure and mark 2½" down on each long side and toward the center on the short end of one end of the pieced strip as shown in Figure 2.

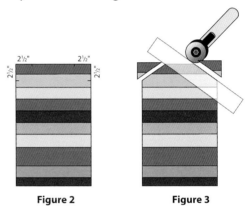

Figure 2   Figure 3

4. Align a ruler with the marks and trim off the corners to create the flap end of the card keeper as shown in Figure 3.

5. Repeat steps 3 and 4 with lining and batting pieces.

6. Pin the ends of the rickrack to the center of the right side of the flap end of the card keeper top to form a loop as shown in Figure 4; stitch in place. ***Note:*** *Adjust the size of the loop to fit your button, if necessary.*

Figure 4

7. Layer and pin the pieced card keeper top right sides together with the lining piece and place on the batting. Stitch all around the edges, leaving the straight 8½" end open as shown in Figure 5 on page 154.

8. Trim corners and turn right side out, pushing out points at corners. Press edges flat.

9. Fold the raw edges of the open end to the inside ¼", press and stitch ⅛" from edge as shown in Figure 6.

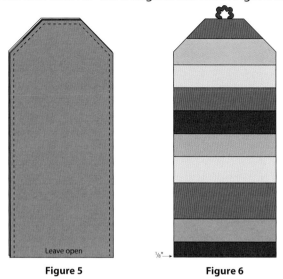

Figure 5   Figure 6

10. Referring to Figure 7, fold up the bottom end 6¼" and fold the flap end down. Using the rickrack loop as a guide, mark the button location.

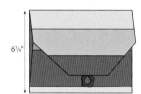

Figure 7

11. Unfold and sew button in place where marked, stitching through the batting and lining.

12. Fold again as in step 10, leaving top flap open, and stitch side edges together to secure pocket. Topstitch flap close to the edges to finish.

CARDS

MATERIALS

4 blank cards with envelopes
Assorted fabric scraps
Assorted ribbon, lace and rickrack scraps
Assorted buttons
Scrapbook adhesive or glue stick
Lightweight fusible adhesive

Cards General Instructions

1. Prepare fabric scraps for use on the cards by bonding lightweight fusible web to the wrong side of the fabric scraps before cutting into shapes as directed by manufacturer's instructions.

2. Referring to photos of sample cards as examples, arrange design elements on the card fronts.

3. When satisfied with placement of items, glue or fuse in place as directed with adhesive or fusible product instructions.

4. When dry or cooled, insert cards and envelopes into the card keeper for safe storage until ready to use or give as gifts. ■

Designer's Tip

Use motifs from the fabric used in the card keeper on the cards to make coordinated sets. In the sample shown, one of the flowers from the large floral fabric was used to make a matching card. Simply apply fusible adhesive to the fabric, select and cut out the shape, remove the paper from the cut shape and position and fuse to the paper.

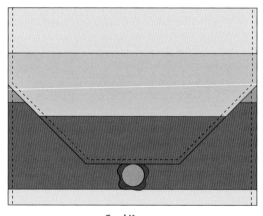

Card Keeper
Placement Diagram Approximately 8" x 6½"

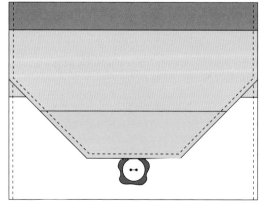

Second Card Keeper
Placement Diagram Approximately 8" x 6½"

Patchwork Pincushions

Showcase a centerpiece on your holiday table with this pretty topper.

DESIGNS BY CHRIS MALONE

PROJECT SPECIFICATIONS

Skill Level: Beginner
Pincushion Size: 6" x 6"

MATERIALS

Assorted bright-color scraps—12 for Rail Fence and 4
    for Pinwheel
Scrap white for Pinwheel
2 (7") squares low-loft batting
Thread
Extra-strong thread
4 assorted colors and white size 12–16 pearl cotton
Fiberfill
3–4 assorted-size coordinating buttons for each
    pincushion
Basic sewing tools and supplies

Cutting

1. From assorted bright-color scraps, cut 12 (1½" x 3½")
assorted C rectangles, 4 (3½") assorted D squares and
1 (6½") backing square.

2. Cut 4 (3⅞") assorted bright-color squares. Subcut
each square in half on 1 diagonal to make 8 B
triangles. Set aside 1 triangle of each color for another
project.

3. Cut 2 (3⅞") white scrap squares; subcut each square
in half on 1 diagonal to make 4 A triangles.

Completing the Rail Fence Pincushion

1. Arrange and join the 12 C rectangles in four sets of
three C units each referring to Figure 1.

Make 4

Figure 1

2. Arrange and join the C units in two rows of two
units each, alternating the direction of the units as
shown in Figure 2 to complete the pieced top.

Figure 2

3. Pin or baste the pieced top right side up on a
batting square. Hand-quilt a line down the center
of each C rectangle, using a different-color thread in
each C unit.

4. When quilting is complete, trim batting even with
the edges of the pieced top.

5. Pin the quilted top and the backing square right
sides together and sew all around, leaving a 2"
opening along one side for turning. Trim corners and
turn right side out.

6. Stuff with fiberfill through the opening until the
pincushion is full, but not overly firm.

7. Fold in the opening seam allowance; hand-stitch
opening closed to finish the pincushion.

8. Thread a needle with a doubled length of extra-
strong thread and make a substantial knot at the end.

9. Insert the needle into the
top center through to the
back center. Add a button
to the back and come back
up to the center front. Pull
to indent the pincushion
and knot the thread to hold.
Add a stack of two or three
buttons in varying sizes and
colors with the largest on the
bottom as shown in Figure 3.

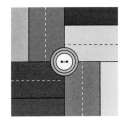

Figure 3

10. Go back through the pincushion and back button. Sew back and forth a few times, knot thread and trim to finish as shown in Figure 4.

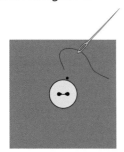

Figure 4

Completing the Pinwheel Pincushion

1. Place an A triangle right sides together with a B triangle and stitch on the diagonal side to make an A-B unit as shown in Figure 5. Repeat to make a total of four A-B units.

Make 4

Figure 5

2. Arrange and join two A-B units to make a row; repeat and join rows to complete the pieced top as shown in Figure 6.

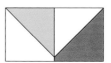

Figure 6

3. Join the four D squares to make the pincushion backing as shown in Figure 7.

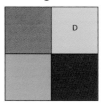

Figure 7

4. Pin or baste the pieced top on a batting square. Use white pearl cotton to hand-quilt ¼" from seams as shown in Figure 8.

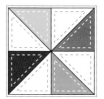

Figure 8

5. Complete the pincushion referring to steps 4–10 of Completing the Rail Fence Pincushion to complete the Pinwheel Pincushion. ■

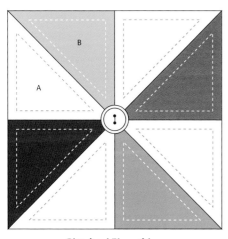

Pinwheel Pincushion
Placement Diagram 6" x 6"

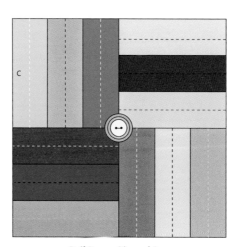

Rail Fence Pincushion
Placement Diagram 6" x 6"

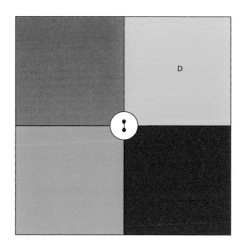

Pinwheel Pincushion Back
Placement Diagram 6" x 6"

Project Gallery

Burst of Color, 4

Gettysburg Revisited, 8

Rules of Chaos, 12

Concrete Jungle, 17

African Sunset, 20

The Romance of Camelot, 25

Christmas Hospitality Runner, 29

Flourish Christmas Table Runner, 32

Angels Among Us, 35

Old St. Nick, 44

Bull's-Eye, 51

Holiday Joy, 40

Piece-Full Days, 56

The Colors of Butterfly Wings, 60

Old-Fashioned Rose Patch, 66

Happy Scrappy Houses, 69

Memories, 74

Black & White Sawtooth, 78

Peaches & Cream, 82

Yukon, 85

Cross Ties, 90

Fractured Stars, 94

Pedaling Petals, 98

Yo-Yo Bedwarmer, 102

Almost Amish, 106

Forever Spring Bed Runner, 110

Free-Falling Leaves Dining Set, 114

Twist 'n' Spin Place Mats, 118

Green Tea Place Mats & Hot Pads, 121

Autumn Ties Table Mat, 124

Scrappy Heart Candle Mat, 128

Selvage Backpack, 131

County Fair Trio, 138

Bottle & Cup Wraps, 144

Clever Clutch 148

Patchwork Pincushions, 155

Card Keeper & Matching Cards, 152

Finishing Your Quilt

1. Press quilt top on both sides; check for proper seam pressing and trim all loose threads.

2. Sandwich batting between the stitched top and the prepared backing piece; pin or baste layers together to hold. Mark quilting design and quilt as desired by hand or machine.

3. When quilting is complete, remove pins or basting. Trim batting and backing fabric edges even with raw edges of quilt top.

4. Join binding strips on short ends with diagonal seams to make one long strip; trim seams to ¼" and press seams open.

5. Fold the binding strip in half with wrong sides together along length; press.

6. Sew binding to quilt edges, matching raw edges, mitering corners and overlapping ends.

7. Fold binding to the back side and stitch in place to finish. ∎

Special Thanks

Please join us in thanking the talented designers and quilters below.

Cheryl Adam
The Romance of Camelot, 25

Kathy Brown
Cross Ties, 90

Lucy A. Fazely & Michael L. Burns
African Sunset, 20
Yukon, 85

Gina Gempesaw
Bottle & Cup Wraps, 144
Concrete Jungle, 17
County Fair Trio, 138

Bev Getschel
Memories, 74

Cara Gulati
Pedaling Petals, 98

Sandra L. Hatch
Black & White Sawtooth, 78

Connie Kauffman
Autumn Ties Table Mat, 124
Gettysburg Revisited, 8
Green Tea Place Mats & Hot Pads, 121
Happy Scrappy Houses, 69

Debby Kratovil
Burst of Color, 4

Kate Laucomer
Fractured Stars, 94

Chris Malone
Angels Among Us, 35
Free-Falling Leaves Dining Set, 114
Old St. Nick, 44
Patchwork Pincushions, 155
Yo-Yo Bedwarmer, 102

Tricia Lynn Maloney
Card Keeper & Matching Cards, 152
Twist 'n' Spin Place Mats, 118

Rochelle Martin
Old-Fashioned Rose Patch, 66
Scrappy Heart Candle Mat, 128

Cynthia Myerberg
Rules of Chaos, 12

Christine A. Schultz
Selvage Backpack, 131

Ruth Ann Sheffield
Piece-Full Days, 56

Wendy Sheppard
Christmas Hospitality Runner, 29

Joyce Stewart
The Colors of Butterfly Wings, 60

Cate Tallman-Evans
Almost Amish, 106

Carolyn S. Vagts
Flourish Christmas Table Runner, 32
Forever Spring Bed Runner, 110
Holiday Joy, 40
Peaches & Cream, 82

Lynn Weglarz
Clever Clutch, 148

Jean Ann Wright
Bull's Eye, 51